THE EASY WAY TO START
SMOKING

THE EASY WAY TO START
SMOKING

GEORGE COCKERILL & DAVID OWEN

CANONGATE

Edinburgh · New York · Melbourne

We are grateful to everyone who buys this book and tolerant of library readers. However, it is you that will be thanking us in three weeks' time. So, in advance, all we can say is…you're welcome!

The authors

First published in Great Britain in 2005 by Robson Books, The Chrysalis Building, Bramley Road, London W10 6SP

THE PUBLISHER MAINTAINS THAT SMOKING IS HARMFUL TO YOU AND THOSE AROUND YOU AND MAY CAUSE SERIOUS ILLNESS. THE PUBLISHER DISCLAIMS ALL RESPONSIBILITY FOR YOUR PERSONAL ACTIONS AND DOES NOT ENDORSE SMOKING IN ANY WAY. THIS BOOK SHOULD BE READ AS FRIVOLOUS LIGHTHEARTED FUN WITH THE FULL UNDERSTANDING OF THE REALITIES OF SMOKING AS A SIGNIFICANT ISSUE THAT MAY HAVE MANY LONG-TERM SIDE EFFECTS. THIS BOOK IS NOT RECOMMENDED FOR INDIVIDUALS UNDER THE AGE OF SIXTEEN.

Printed in the United States of America

FIRST AMERICAN EDITION

ISBN-10: 1-84195-744-5

ISBN-13: 978-1-84195-744-9

Original book design by Tara O'Leary
Additional illustrations by Kang Chen

Canongate
841 Broadway
New York, NY 10003

06 07 08 09 10   10 9 8 7 6 5 4 3 2 1

WHO SHOULD READ THIS BOOK?

The answer is easy and all-inclusive. Anyone who wants to start smoking and stay smoking. Anyone who already smokes but wants to smoke more, or needs to be sure that it isn't just a passing fad but is indeed a lifelong habit that they will never be without.

If you smoke but have friends and relatives who haven't started or perhaps have even given up, you will find in this book a whole host of useful things to say and do to help them. You may even be thinking of buying this book as a present—perhaps it was included on a friend's Christmas or birthday list, or maybe they just asked for a pack of cigarettes and you don't think they are quite ready for them. Either way, you can be sure that this book is a gift that will keep on giving. And while no one should be in the business of giving just to receive something in return, you may want to turn down a corner or place a bookmark with your return address on page 54, where your friend will find a picture of our fantastic "Nothing's Gonna Stop Us Now" T-shirts ($25). Let's hope they get the message.

In short, everyone should read this book and you are all so very welcome to it and the bounty it will bring.

CONTENTS

CONTENTS

CONTENTS

THE EASY WAY TO START
SMOKING

PART ONE
THE LIGHT OF YOUR LIFE

"I have nothing to declare except my cigarettes."
—Oscar Wilde

So, You Want to Start Smoking?

You do? Great! It may not be obvious to you now, but already you have taken a big step closer to achieving your new habit. Just by buying this book you have admitted to yourself that there is something wrong in your life. That your life without cigarettes is unsatisfying and pointless. You are in the zone. What's more, if you order one of our exclusive "L-Plate" T-shirts, you could soon be sitting for a few minutes in the smoking section at one of the many participating restaurants across the country. You may not smoke yet, but you can get a taste for its privileges. Follow this book to the letter and in just four weeks you won't need a big red "L" printed on your shirt to hang out on the fire escape at work—the lit cig hanging from your mouth (and the slight yellowing of your fingertips) will be all the ID you need to show!

If you are at all unsure of your mental commitment at this stage, ask yourself:

Do I want to smoke?

☐ Yes ☐ No

Do I really want to smoke?

☐ Yes ☐ No

If you answered yes to either question you are on the right track. If you answered no, then you need to take a long hard look at yourself in the mirror.

Do you see a smoker looking back at you?

☐ Yes ☐ No

You have to want to start. We claim a 95 percent success rate at our nationwide clinics but we can't and won't help anyone who hasn't already convinced themselves that they need to develop a chronic nicotine habit. Have you? If you don't really want to smoke, this book will be of no use to you whatsoever. You may as well throw it out of the window onto the street below. Alternatively, take it back with the receipt and exchange it for our other recently published title, *Aaaargh! Which Is the Right Self-help Book for Me?*

Still with us? Good. Best to shake off the "just curious" types early on, and the slow readers will catch up with us in their own time.

This is the first chapter of your new life. We have carefully outlined a course to prepare you for the inevitable—smoking! There is a lot of information to absorb but also some fun exercises to try out. If it all feels a bit too much like school, don't forget that in later chapters you can always nip around the back of the bike sheds for a quick smoke. You may even find us there!

To keep in step with our patented Kick Start program, we recommend that you spend three days on each of the sections. Of course, you can reread the pages as often as your schedule or concentration allows. You may even be reading this paragraph for the third or fourth time—in which case you really should get on with it.

This is it. Here we go.

Good luck! (You won't need it!!)

It's OK—
I'll Start Tomorrow

Yeah, yeah. But didn't you say that yesterday? And the day before that? At seminars and book readings people often ask us: When is the right time to start? Our reply is always the same—NOW! (At really big corporate training sessions we will really shout that out!) Quite simply, the sooner you start, the sooner you will gain the benefits of being a smoker. How many non-smokers have you heard say

- "I'll start tomorrow."
- "I'll start after Lent."
- "I'll start when there's been a death in the family."

These are all classic delaying excuses. Is that what you want? Do you want to start smoking tomorrow? Really? Perhaps you want to stop reading this book now. Is it time for bed? Well, goodnight John Boy, and sweet dreams.

What? Still here? Couldn't do it, could you? You had to read on and we are glad you did.

Over and over again you will have heard your mother say things like "Why put off until tomorrow what you can do today?" Well, you may not have been man enough to admit it until now but, damn it, she was right. That's why, just three weeks after you have started reading this book, you will be smoking, and maybe even enjoying, your first cigarette!

EXERCISE 1

Doing something today you could have put off until tomorrow

This is a simple exercise that your friends may find crazy —but don't let that stop you from practicing.

Get into bed. Almost fall asleep. Now get up again and clean your teeth! That's right! Mad, isn't it?

Try this for two days, perhaps even progressing to having a shower and getting fully dressed in your work clothes before undressing and getting back into bed for the night.

Note: Under no circumstances should you make the mistake of putting this whole exercise off until the next day. Only the unemployable and actors get up, get dressed and go back to bed in the morning.

Commit Yourself

Do you really want to start? This is a decision you have to take for yourself. If you received this book as a gift, have a quick think to yourself—who wants me to start smoking? Me, or the kind person who gave me the book? If you are in any doubt, put this book away, go into town and buy it again—for yourself, with your own money. If you have a problem with that suggestion, then perhaps you should consider that it is not actually you that wants to start. You may be the victim of peer pressure.

What Is Peer Pressure?

Maybe you are only attempting to start because of someone else. It could be your parents who are desperate for you to start. Maybe your new smoking boyfriend or girlfriend doubts your commitment to the relationship. Whoever it is and however respected a position they may hold in the community, you must realize that the only person who can get you started is you.

In our clinics we have treated a number of people in recent years who have entered into a relationship on the Internet and have somewhat embellished the truth when describing themselves. "Oh yes," they confidently type, "I'm a forty a day man. Marlboro Red soft packs—they go so well with my vintage red soft top sports car." Next thing they know, they are due to meet their true love at the immigration center and they panic. The fact that Shiang-Lee has a mustache only makes her look more angry when they fumble around trying to find the ashtray in their mustard-yellow Nissan Altra for the first time. That's when they come to us. When they realize that this smoking thing is not something they can just play at. Because they would be playing with fire.

The Choice Is Yours

After you have officially started, you might find that a smart aleck friend will say, "Oh! I see you're not smoking now! I thought you said you were a smoker!" Don't be put off. Brief relapses are bound to happen. Remember, soon you will be able to simply smile, light a cigarette and reply, "See! I can start whenever I want to!"

If you live in an Amish community or are already hospitalized, friends and family may try to tempt you away from your smoking goal. It will make your clothes stink, they will say. It will ruin your sense of taste and smell, they will cry. It will give you cancer, they may shout. And they will be right.

In these trying times, try breathing deeply and saying this to yourself:

> *I am going to be a smoker. I will smoke because I will be deeply addicted. I have heard it may kill me, but I have made a personal choice to deny this. I admit I am often tempted not to start at all, but when I finally do light up, this feeling will quickly go away.*

Later, you may encounter those who are jealous of the ruthless abandon with which you leap from ten to twenty to thirty a day in a matter of weeks, but do not be put off. See our later chapter: "How to Argue with Nonsmokers and Win Every Time."

Get the Habit!

Let's look at the two key habits that we'll be concentrating on in this book:

- The physical habit of addiction
- The psychological habit of smoking

It's easy in your early smoking days to forget that you are a smoker. No one is going to call you up every fifteen minutes to remind you to smoke. A few hours may pass by without you chancing upon an ad for cigarettes to prompt you back into action. In fact, you may be seeing such ads all the time but are not yet able to distinguish them as anything other than relatively harmless postmodern visual puns. At the end of such a day, you may find yourself thinking, "I have only smoked two cigarettes today. I may as well give up!" During these difficult first weeks, the addictive properties of nicotine will be your friend—an automatic alarm to remind you to keep smoking.

EXERCISE 2

Making a commitment to something that may kill you

Luckily for you this exercise is more of a game. You may have heard of it. It is called Russian Roulette. It is a game of chance for one or more players . . .

"Hang on!" you may be thinking, that game is dangerous. It involves one or more players. And it involves a loaded gun and could kill me. I don't even have a gun. Do I have to go out and buy a gun as well now?

Well, no you don't. But we did want you to think about guns, bullets, and about life and death for just a second. Was it a nasty trick to pull? Maybe, but also a valuable one. It was real. It is your new reality.

That's it. That's the exercise for this section done. Now breathe a sigh of relief.

Ah! you may ask, if it is that easy, why the two bullet points?

A good question. Sadly, nicotine is not as addictive as you might think. Even experienced smokers can manage up to an hour and a half (mostly at the movies or when swimming) without nicotine. This is why we will be working equally hard on the psychological habit too. From the second you light up your first cigarette, not only is the addiction already beginning to form, but you will also discover a natural affinity with the procedure and paraphernalia of smoking.

Nonsmokers often complain that they just don't know what to do with their hands. They find that washing an apple or opening a bottle of iced tea just isn't enough. As a smoker, you won't have this problem. You will use your hands to open packs of cigarettes, to hold cigarettes; even, perhaps, to cup matches in the wind. After a few days you will find that the actual addiction to cigarettes pretty much looks after itself.

But I Can't Afford It!

It's true—you need to put a great deal of time and effort into starting smoking. But think about it—there are very few worthwhile things in your life that haven't required your energy and dedication. Jimi Hendrix (thirty-five cigarettes a day) didn't learn to play like that overnight, you know!

Experienced smokers set their daily budget for smoking at around $25 per day. But let's not try to run before we can walk! To begin with, you will need just $7.95 per day to get the habit. This may sound like a lot of money—but just think of the things you won't be able to afford merely by directing your income toward cigarettes. Here are some things that cost the same, but which you will no longer need or be able to buy!

- A CD single by a chart-topping band
- Two CD singles by Dave Mathews
- A weeklong DVD rental of *Turner & Hooch*

And as you smoke more and more, the cost mounts up. After just a couple of weeks you will be unable to afford clothes from Men's Warehouse or Kohl's. Pretty soon even a Saturn with cloth seats will be beyond your grasp.

But where will the money come from? Not buying other things is all very well but such a method only works if you have the money in the first place. What if you have nothing? What if you are unemployable or too lazy to work? After considering this problem for many years, we have come to the conclusion that the only legal way to acquire money without

EXERCISE 3

Understanding the real value of money

Ask an experienced smoker what they could buy with $8 and they will quickly answer—"a pack of cigs." How do they do that? We will teach you.

Simply practice these questions a few times until you have learned the answers (which you will not find in the back of the book) or calculated them for yourself.

- How many packs of twenty cigarettes can you buy for $8?
- How many can you buy for $75?
- How many can you buy for $750?
- How many cartons is that?

Hang on a minute, you may be thinking, this is the same boring math that I did in school. Well, yes it is and no it isn't. By learning these simple sums you are overdeveloping parts of the brain that smokers need to use every day. It is an example of a technique that we like to call "Mental Arithmetic."

working or inheriting it is to search for loose change down the backs of sofas.

Truly—it is the only honest way.

It is well worth conducting thorough and regular searches behind settee cushions, and such forays should by no means be limited to your own home. A friend's couch can be furtively explored without suspicion while holding a perfectly convincing conversation, or by deliberately dropping a small but imprecise amount of your own money and openly searching for it.

On a grander scale, a trip to the local OTB just before closing time on a Saturday can often net a quantity of small change more commonly associated with a big win at the track. Care should always be taken when reaching down the back of sofa beds, particularly those that are self-assembled and have been known to snare the unwary like giant human mousetraps. In your own home it is well worth making a few minor alterations to your furniture to maximize your potential gain. The discreet placing of a telephone directory under the front of your sofa cushions increases the incline of the average cushion by around ten degrees. This will shift and displace the round, rolling coins, freeing them from friends' pockets.

Only Fools Rush In

We know that if you have read this far you are desperate to start smoking. Who can blame you? You have been going cold turkey your entire life! Frustrated? Well, hold on to that feeling. We can work with it. But let's take this one step at a time, shall we? "How Soon Is Now," sang the Eighties indie band The Smiths. Too soon by far, is our answer.

You have probably already tried every method to start smoking: hypnosis, acupuncture, predilection therapy and good old Mr. Will Power. You may even have thought to yourself how easy it would be to simply buy a pack and a box of matches. If only it were that simple!

This book is entitled *The Easy Way to Start Smoking* but just look at how many pages there are yet to read. That's right—lots.

How many times have you heard nonsmokers say something like, "I tried smoking when I was a teenager but I coughed my guts up and never tried it again" or, "I used to smoke but it was so expensive I gave it up"? These are people who had a choice and, at the time, really thought that they wanted to become smokers. They had no approach, no methodology and evidently no best-selling self-help book called *The Easy Way to Start Smoking* on their library shelves.

If you want to start smoking and stay smoking properly, you are going to have to make some changes in your "nonsmoking" life. You need to change your social routine and your working habits.

Try at all times to be where smokers are. Spend time in bars and coffee shops. Avoid places like gyms and gas stations. You may even wish to take a short break in France or Japan. Just as nonsmokers will enjoy a gastronomic tour of Italy, beginners and experienced smokers alike will savor a smoking holiday in Russia or Poland.

Even your TV viewing habits will affect your smoking. No one smokes on *Will and Grace,* for example. Filmwise, if you're watching Disney instead of Humphrey Bogart, you have a problem. Try calling in sick to work and watching some classic movies in the afternoon. In many of the old black-and-white flicks the smoking scenes are for real—they aren't even acting!

A more innovative way to get into the swing of things is to join a local dramatic society and get yourself cast in the role of heavy smoker (see "Busman's Holiday" in our Glossary). Most plays and musicals have such a part, and if not, you can always justify your interpretation of a chain-smoking Mary Poppins on artistic grounds, especially if you have a voice like Bonnie Tyler's. Such theatrical pursuits not only have the benefit of demanding heavy smoking during performances and rehearsals but, of course, most actors are notorious puffers who will actually congratulate you, hug you and call you "darling" each time you light up.

You should also be sure to make the necessary changes in your home. Try leaving packs of cigarettes and boxes of matches around the house as a useful reminder to spark up.

Make sure you place a few packs in drawers and cupboards that you haven't looked in for years—when you eventually find them in such unlikely places it will seem like fate itself must have put them there!

Ensure each room has a good number of ashtrays. It's tempting to say to yourself, "Well, there's no ashtray here, I may as well not have a cigarette." You could try slipping a bent feng shui expert a few extra bucks to reorganize your home and maximize the temptation. Finally, if you can afford it, we would also strongly advise moving house to be nearer to a twenty-four-hour garage if at all possible.

The Trigger Theory

The oldest question in the world is: "What came first? The chicken or the egg?" In the world of smoking theory the question most often asked is: "What came first? The cigarette or a good shag?"

You may already have heard of the phenomenon that is the "Post-Coital Cigarette." There is nothing better than reclining in a lover's arms and enjoying a good smoke—although the sex itself may run the experience a close second. One day a week we sublet the meeting rooms at our clinics to marriage guidance counselors and have been known to offer a little advice of our own. We talk about how to avoid the urge to spark up too soon when having sex. We recommend trying to focus on something completely removed from smoking—the small of your lover's back, perhaps, or a porn film you may once have seen. Of course, you may only just be old enough to make love. The age at which you are legally allowed to have sex is the same as that for smoking. Do remember that while your deli guy is legally obliged to sell you a pack of Camels on your sixteenth birthday, they probably won't sleep with you.

EXERCISE 4

Weaning yourself on to cigarettes

Over the next few days, we suggest you try out a little program of replacement therapy. Just as methadone works for wannabe smack addicts, the suggestions below can help you too.

- Bite your nails
- Chew ordinary gum
- Chew nicotine gum
- Apply nicotine patches to your body
- Suck on a plastic inhaler or "dummy" cigarette
- Drop to your knees and weep

Stresses and Strains

It has also been well documented that being stressed makes people want to smoke. This is not to say that you should put yourself in difficult or dangerous situations just for the hell of it. Should you ever find yourself in the armed forces and fighting behind enemy lines, it may be tempting to reach for a cigarette. The enemy can smell fear, you reason, and a smoke will calm and soothe me. While that is true, they can also detect a naked flame from space. No one should think they can outrun or hide from a heat-seeking missile.

One technique for inducing pressure or panic is to tell yourself you have developed cancer in an important part of your body. Convince yourself and you will be so unnerved that a cigarette may seem the only way out. It may amuse you to note that this same technique is also used by those who wish to give up smoking!

You might also like to try hanging around churches on Sundays in the hope of catching a funeral. You have a legal right to attend any funeral and you will find that the atmosphere on exiting the church is most conducive to a few puffs. Should you be lucky enough to actually know, or even to have loved the deceased, you will find that your sense of grief is immeasurably increased.

EXERCISE 5

Reminding yourself to smoke

For this exercise you will need a cooking pan, a water supply and a few dozen eggs.

Imagine that you are a smoker and enjoying a cigarette. Now pour water into the pan and bring to boil. Carefully place an egg into the pan and cook until completely hard boiled. Approximately eight minutes will have elapsed. If you were a smoker, now would be the time to light up again.

Repeat the exercise as necessary throughout the day. Think of something to do with the eggs.

The First Purchase

It is quite possible to begin smoking without actually buying cigarettes. How many times have you been offered a cigarette in the past but had to refuse it on the grounds that you don't smoke? We know the answer and, yes, it is a crying shame. However, even with just over a week to go before you start handing over your own cash, you can make the most of other people's generosity.

Try standing close to smokers and engaging them in conversation. Don't be scared, they are just like you and us (well, more like us, in that they smoke—but not too different in any other way). Don't actually ask for a cigarette—wait until you are offered one. In later chapters we will advise you on how to ask for and actually receive a cigarette from almost anyone. At this stage we don't want you to smoke the cigarette, so asking would just be rude. If and when you are offered a cigarette, simply place it behind your ear and mutter that you are "keeping it for later" (see "Aunt Sally" in our Glossary).

Now walk away and discreetly place the cigarette in a prepared container with hardened edges so that it doesn't get damaged. It may not surprise you that an empty cigarette pack will make the perfect receptacle. You can now sidle up to another group of smokers and try your luck again. If by the end of the evening you have more than, say, three cigarettes, you might practice offering one to someone else. Not only will this be laying the groundwork for exercises in later chapters but it will, in a small but not insignificant way, contribute to the general spirit of camaraderie between smokers that made this exercise possible in the first place.

Sooner or later, however, you will need to buy some cigarettes. Other people's smokes (OPs) are not to be relied upon and you have no control over brand or strength.

Where to Buy

Supermarkets appear to offer great value but you will invariably find yourself at the rear of a slow, shuffling line of old people handing in lottery tickets that look for all the world like winners until they are examined by the checkout girl and rejected twice by the machine.

You may be tempted to try vending machines. Unfortunately, a levy of four cigarettes will be imposed and you will have to make do with sixteen cigarettes and a pack that rattles.

All new smokers are advised against making their first purchase from a specialist tobacconist. The range on offer will bewilder you and these establishments rarely sell normal cigarettes. They specialize in retailing products such as kiwi-and-banana-flavored pipe tobacco and other products that have probably twice outlived their sell-by dates.

Steer clear too of any shop located within five miles of your house or place of work. Screw up your debut order and you may be too embarrassed to return and will be forced to travel long distances to stock up in the future.

If you do make your first purchase at an ordinary news-stand you will be confronted by a multitude of brands and flavors. Don't panic. This short guide will prepare you:

Buying Cigarettes—the Facts

Lights
Contrary to popular belief, these don't weigh any less than regular cigarettes—and no, you don't get free matches! Nor are they intended for dieting smokers (although smoking is a great way to lose weight). Light cigarettes are simply cigarettes with less tar and are suitable for waif-like models or people with flu.

Menthol Cigarettes
These are mint-flavored cigarettes popular with actresses and those with sore throats. Also a handy short cut to minty fresh breath if you've not had time to clean your teeth. If your grandma kisses you at Christmas, it is wise to smoke a menthol cigarette before and after the event.

Soft Packs
It's tempting to flash these around when trying to impress more experienced smokers. But don't bother, people will just think you're taking a year off before you start college. Also, you run the risk of compressing your cigs and making for a slower smoke. And remember, slower smokes mean less smokes which could do a great deal of harm to your Daily Amount.

Duty-Free Cigarettes
It's a common misconception that the huge cigarette cartons found in duty-free shops contain enormous cigarettes. If only. No, they simply contain two hundred ordinary cigarettes.

Still a bit nervous? We're not at all surprised. The first request can be difficult. What if you accidentally ask for twenty packs of cigarettes? Would you have the cash to cover your mistake? Will people in the line behind you start sniggering? Doubtless they will. We strongly suggest that you distract attention from your cigarette order by purchasing a few other items at the same time: a copy of *Asian Babes,* perhaps, and a pack of extra-strong condoms. Then simply approach the counter, breathe out, relax and say, "Marlboro Lights, please."

There. You've done it! You have bought a pack of cigarettes.

Your First Cigarette

Where did you lose your virginity? In front of your parents? In a crowded bar? In the parking lot of your local convenience store? Of course not!

Smoking your first cigarette is no different. It is just as intimate, and will probably last twice as long.

At our seminars we recommend all sorts of places as the ideal locations for kicking off your habit: park benches, bus stops, train stations after 11 p.m. If you are unsure, look down at the ground. Can you see evidence of other people smoking? Is there a butt under your foot? Yes? Good. You are home.

Now for a really important point:

Have you got your cigarettes?

If you can crack this early on, then you're on to a winner. And before we go on:

Have you got a light?

There is quite simply no smoke without fire.

You have? Great. It is now our pleasure to ask you, for the first of what we hope will be many times, "Would you like a cigarette?"

Let's do it.

Tear off the cellophane on the pack and open the lid. Follow the instructions printed on the foil and "Pull." Take out your first cigarette, hold it and look at it.

You may now wish to read the next line and, if you think you have got it, put the book down.

Put the filter end of the cigarette in your mouth.

How does that feel? You're a little nervous perhaps, but isn't the overwhelming sensation one of confidence and control?

Light the end of the cigarette and suck gently. Smoke will be drawn out of the cigarette and flow effortlessly into your lungs. Fantastic.

Don't be alarmed if you don't feel addicted yet. The craving for your second cigarette will not come until after you have completely finished the first and even then will take a little time to form.

And don't panic about your body's reaction to smoking. Coughing and giddiness are common responses. Your eyes may water but with any luck this will be caused not only by your new friend smoke, but also by tears of joy at finally getting the habit!

GREAT NEWS.
YOU HAVE SMOKED YOUR FIRST CIGARETTE.

BETTER NEWS.
THERE ARE NINETEEN MORE IN THE PACK!

The Marriage Vows

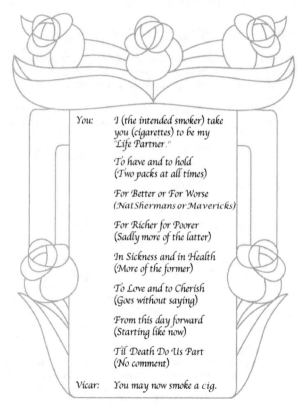

You: I (the intended smoker) take
you (cigarettes) to be my
"Life Partner."

To have and to hold
(Two packs at all times)

For Better or For Worse
(Nat Shermans or Mavericks)

For Richer for Poorer
(Sadly more of the latter)

In Sickness and in Health
(More of the former)

To Love and to Cherish
(Goes without saying)

From this day forward
(Starting like now)

Til Death Do Us Part
(No comment)

Vicar: You may now smoke a cig.

Your New Year's Resolution

It is the most popular time of the year to start. January first is the one calendar date when hundreds of thousands of people reach for a pack of smokes, strike a match and give it a whirl.

Of course, by the first week of February the vast majority have lapsed and returned to their nonsmoking habits. A colleague at work will have tired of their new regime of staying in watching television and will have suggested going down to the gym. The new smoker will join them out of sympathy. They'll slip into their sweatpants and that will be it, back on the treadmill for the rest of the year.

The truth of the matter is that New Year just isn't the best time to start. There is far too much pressure surrounding the event. It's too public. Everyone in your family will know that you are trying to start and you'll feel as if you have let them down as much as yourself if you can't keep it up. You are far better off starting on a totally nondescript, average day—like next Wednesday—and quietly getting on with it. If, however, you really feel it would help to set a date and make something of your smoking debut, here are a few suggestions that do work.

The First Day of a Vacation

Getting out of your nonsmoking office environment is just what you need and the duty-free start is highly recommended. Not only are the cigarettes cheaper but they are in plentiful supply. If you can get through four hundred smokes on a weekend in Bermuda, you'll do fine. Pick up your full quota again on the way back and you'll feel duty bound to keep smoking for at least another two months.

Bonfire Night

Look! You can write your name in the air!

Your Birthday

Don't add to the peer pressure by letting everyone know what you are up to. Try asking your mom for a lighter, your brother or sister for an ashtray, and your grandma for $5. No need to have a party—just stay in and play with your new toys.

National No-Smoking Day

Everyone loves a smart-ass.

On the Release of a New Pop Single

Determine to have a cig every time you hear a certain song being played on radio or TV. The heavy airplay of "Smells Like Teen Spirit" worked great for Arnold Dellar of Iowa until he died after the track's 22,393rd play on college radio.

February 29th

Avoid this day as you'll only be able to have your smoking birthday party every four years.

Alternative Methodologies

This book will get you there. We are in no doubt about that. Think of us as the drivers of a bus that, although it will wind its way all around the houses and stop every quarter of a mile to pick up new passengers and let a few losers off, will still, after just three weeks on board, drop you at the shops where you can buy some cigarettes. Anyone can ride the bus—we just don't sell return tickets!

Despite the indisputable evidence that this book is by far the best way to catch the smoking bug, other practitioners continue to advertise their services. Many of these more alternative methodologies you will recognize from the cheaply printed cards stuck on the inside of health food store windows—others actually have some validity. If you are tempted to try any of the following, read our guide first and consider them only as complementary medicines to the course prescribed in this book.

Hypnosis

"You are feeling sleepy...your eyelids are feeling very heavy...you want a cigarette." Yeah, right. As you will know by now, your desire for a cigarette is at its strongest when you are most awake, nervous and stressed.

Nicotine Gum

Teetotal patients hoping to develop a strong dependency on alcohol often get off to a good start on wine gums. It's not so easy for smokers. Nicotine has a distinctly unpleasant taste when taken orally and the makers of these gums struggle to compete with Wrigleys, Orbit and the other big brands. If patients can get over the taste hurdle, they will at least be getting some nicotine into their blood stream. The problems, however, come later when the patient makes the transition to cigarettes and finds that they have developed completely the wrong mouth action. They are likely to chew the ends of their first few cigs and in some cases will, for the rest of their lives, smoke like a camel. You will recognize these people by the way their mouth moves involuntarily up, down and from side to side, causing the cigarette to flit around like a conductor's baton.

Mediums

Getting in touch with smokers who have passed over to the other side can be inspirational. There is always that little doubt when taking advice from living, breathing smokers that they may not actually be as committed as you. The last thing you want to find is that your smoking guru has suddenly quit and taken up long distance running. Dead smokers know it all. Perhaps you had a grandfather who smoked like a trooper but died years before you were born, or maybe a friend of yours has such an ancestor and wouldn't mind you getting in touch directly.

Shock Therapy

Cash-funded by the private pension companies, the government ran a series of shocking public health films in the late eighties. Nonsmokers were faced with horrific images of useless old people who had never smoked and lived healthy lives for far too long. While a few nonsmokers did take up the habit, the campaign is now credited with kick-starting the pro-euthanasia movement.

Electric Shock Therapy

Electrocution can cause people to start smoking but not in the way you might be hoping. As it is, the evidence suggests that more people smoke a cigarette before an electric shock than after. In the U.S. penal system, where electrocution is used as a form of capital punishment, there were forty-nine recorded cases of people having a cigarette before the volts charged through their bodies and none after.

Willpower

This one works! Willpower is the very best way to start smoking outside of actually eating this book. With it you can do pretty much anything. It's not for everyone, though, as this conversation from one of our seminars demonstrates:

Q: How much does it cost?
A: Nothing, not a penny.
Q: Where can I get it?
A: Deep within your soul.
Q: Really?
A: Yes.
Q: Oh. Are you sure I can't buy some?

Group Therapy

"My name is Robert Tandy and I am a nonsmoker." It's been fourteen years since our friend Robert stood up among a group of strangers and made that admission. And four years since he started smoking. It's hard to say if the group therapy worked or if simply spending a decade in the company of a bunch of whining, self-centred nonsmokers drove him to it.

Smoking Techniques for the Beginner

The Classic Two-Finger Grip

It's the same V-sign that the British would use to tell people to fuck off, before MTV, the Blues Brothers and gangsta rappers persuaded everyone that one finger was "like, way cooler." Has the added benefit of being a reverse Churchillian style "V for Victory" sign—an endorsement that you are signalling to yourself every time you light up. In smoking circles there are very few better ways to hold a cigarette than this.

"Smoking's OK with Me!"

By holding a cigarette between your index finger and thumb with the other fingers pointing smartly out, you are able to give the universal "OK" symbol each time you take a drag. Just don't be tempted to try this one in the gay quarter of Havana, Cuba, where the circle made by the thumb and finger is understood to represent the anus and the gesture is an open invitation to any man to bum you.

You CAN do it

Don't worry if after the first few days you still have to concentrate to keep smoking regularly. This is not unusual. The
rigmarole of finding a pack, then a lighter and then an ashtray
may seem a chore now that the initial buzz has gone. Cigarettes
five hundred to one thousand are never going to be quite the
same. Friends and family will have taken your smoking for
granted and might not encourage you or chastise you when you
are not smoking. But let us promise you, it does get easier.

Take it one cigarette at a time and always be aware of the
four barriers to success: boredom, complacency, forgetfulness
and old habits. Know how to defeat them when they come
a-calling:

Boredom

Is your next cig more or less the same as the last? Not at all.
Every cigarette is a source of fascination to the experienced
smoker, but if you've yet to fully form the obsession it can be
hard. Did you know how many lighter-colored flecks there
are on a Silk Cut filter tip? Did you realize that the barcode
on each pack is slightly different? Try to be less busy in other
areas of your life so that you have more time on your hands.
Consider going part time at work, putting a hobby on ice and
cutting out the evening classes.

Complacency

Just because you smoked thirty yesterday doesn't mean
you should only smoke ten today! And don't think that if
you smoke stronger cigarettes you can smoke fewer of them!

Think you've cracked the habit? Think again. Can you honestly answer yes to these seven questions?

1 Do you have pet names for each of the cigarettes in a pack of twenty?
2 When you read about smoking bans do you weep like a baby?
3 Do you leave an unlit cigarette resting on the edge of the hotplate on your bedside table so that you have a lit cig ready for the moment you wake?
4 Do you know the phrases "Twenty cigarettes please," "That's fine, I'll take any brand" and "Are you sure you haven't got any more out back?" in more than ten foreign languages?
5 Do you often find yourself accidentally lighting things that look like cigarettes? Pencils, bread sticks or tampons?
6 Have you given up using ashtrays and installed bar-style flooring in all the rooms of your house?
7 Including the bathroom?

Forgetfulness

Sometimes you might go a whole hour without remembering to have a cigarette. One option is to purchase our special trainer glasses which place the phrase "Have a cig" in front of your eyes for every waking moment. Another idea is to set and reset the alarm on your mobile phone to sound at twenty-minute intervals. This is especially useful in the cinema, where the action on screen can sometimes be quite engrossing or at best distracting.

Old Habits

It's difficult to get out of the old routine, but remember that starting smoking is a big change in your life and you need to adapt. Try getting off the subway or bus one stop before your destination so you can walk the rest of the way while enjoying a cigarette. Or ask your boyfriend or girlfriend to park the car around the corner from your house at the end of a date. If you can afford TiVo you can pause live TV for cigarette breaks. If not, simply tape what you want to see one night and watch it the next night—it's really not that disruptive when you get into the routine. Finally, try skipping dessert in restaurants so you can fit in a few more smokes while your companions are gorging on their tiramisu.

Present this coupon at any of our *KicK Start* Clinic or Smoking road shows to claim your free shirt.

FREE Shirt

Available in low, medium or extralong

PART TWO
DON'T STOP ME NOW

"Let there be a light."
—God

The Complete
Non-Starters

We are often asked if any of our readers or clinic patients were particularly difficult to get started. Well, there were two people who had big problems picking up the habit. Who were they? That's right—us. We were the ones who found it most difficult to get addicted—it was us. Here are our amazing stories.

David Owen's Story

When did I start smoking? At the age of eleven? The age of twelve? Sixteen? Did I start at the age of twenty? Or a year later, aged twenty-one? Was it at the age of thirty that I started smoking? No. None of these ages are correct, although they do all add up to seventy-eight—the length, in millimeters, of a cigarette.

I know your pain. I spent thirty-three years of my life just like you. Jesus had achieved almost all of what he'd set out to do on the earth before I had discovered my purpose in life. I'd tried to start smoking loads of times. I'd often keep it up for weeks but every time I would eventually go round the bend desperately trying to get used to the taste and smell of cigarettes—let alone remember that I smoked at all. I'd kid myself that I could get by on the occasional cigarette at weddings, a cigar at a christening or a roll-up on the stoop after a good night out.

The horrible irony was that I was already an expert puffer by the age of six. I was asthmatic and was ordered by my doctor to use an inhaler at least twenty times a day. Only now do I realize that the skill and timing needed to get a sharp intake of chemicals into my lungs was exactly what would later take me so many years to "learn." If only my doctor had spent the same time and effort he used teaching me to use my inhaler—one hand on the back of my head, the other clamping my mouth shut—on showing me how to learn to inhale the smoke from cigarettes.

Let me be real with you—David Owen isn't my real name. I can't tell you my real name, but our lawyers say that I can reveal that my father was big in the tobacco business (although I cannot reveal which one or where).

My earliest memories are of standing outside the family factory in Winston-Salem, staring up at the sign, painted in letters two feet high: "Pride in Tobacco," I'd overhear workers trudging through the gates, muttering, "Another day, another dollar." Dad would say much the same thing, only the amounts would be bigger.

I spent many beautiful summers at that wonderful factory; running under the machines, chasing rats and collecting butts; fooling around with the machines creating cigarettes eight feet long; passing hazy hours with the weirdos in the testing room; playing with all sorts of strange new mixes of tobacco, asbestos and fiberglass.

One day—I think I was nine—I noticed several of the workers shuffling off mysteriously to a small room hidden in a corner of the factory. The glass was frosted but I could see people were in there talking animatedly.

I soon discovered that this was the one smoke-free room in the factory where the workers could go and forget about the world of work. The moment I set foot inside, a world of healthy living opened out in front of me and I knew that right there I had found the place where I belonged. I immediately ran home to tell my parents about it. They were NOT impressed.

I suppose it was a way of rebelling against my parents. Mom and Dad would rifle through the pockets of my school blazer and find I'd spent all my cigarette money on chewing gum. Often I'd come home from school stinking of mint and would have to craftily chew some nicotine gum, or swap the ten Parliaments they'd packed in my lunchbox for an apple before I could join them in the smoking room.

But I coped. I was young enough and tough enough—I was going to live forever! I could start smoking whenever I wanted! Then the all-night parties and peer pressure started. I'd have to spend hours surrounded by my smoking friends, wondering what was wrong with me that I couldn't even hold a cigarette without feeling dizzy. Girls wouldn't even talk to me—they said my breath smelt of soap dishes.

And that's how I stayed all through my teens. Then I took my first job. I was a creative working in billboard advertising. Cruel fate put me on the Kool and Newport accounts. Of course, I was a massive failure. I look back at those ads now and realize that my mind was clearly on other things. At the time I just couldn't see the benefits to the public of these products.

Then one morning I woke up after a weeklong yoga retreat and I looked out of my window and shouted—"One day I'm going to die! I could die *any day now* without having developed a serious addiction to nicotine!"

I lit my first cigarette straight away and I knew it right there—I was going to be a smoker for the rest of my life. The smoke coursed through my lungs and I immediately went into a coughing fit that ended in my throwing up the previous night's vegan buffet. A great and wonderful weight had been placed on my shoulders and I wanted to tell the whole world: "I AM A SMOKER!"

George Cockerill's Story

My story is the same as David's, but with different names and situations.

Anatomy of a Smoker

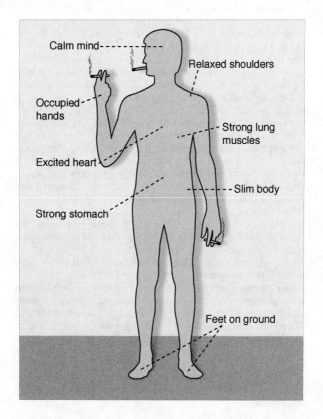

Calm mind

Relaxed shoulders

Occupied hands

Strong lung muscles

Excited heart

Slim body

Strong stomach

Feet on ground

Your Story Is Our Story

At this stage in the book you will have come to realize that you are not alone in your struggle. Even if you live in the furthest outpost of the most remotest part of Alaska and ordered this book via Amazon, you will probably be aware that you are not the only person desperately trying to start smoking—although you may be the only person still waiting for the new Tears For Fears album.

There are literally millions of people around the world trying to get the habit. All these people's experiences are different, yet essentially the same—apart from in Japan, where due to an unchecked shipment of import copies being read from the back to the front, four thousand unlucky Japanese abruptly started smoking heavily and then quit completely en masse three weeks later.

Many of our readers write to us, offering their experiences firsthand. Frequently, these people rather pedantically point out grammatical, spelling and conceptual errors in the text, while others tell us yet again that when they asked for this book they were shown to the humor section. However, some of the letters are so instructive and enlightening that we thought we would share them with you.

Clare - 25	Marcus - 54
"I'm of petite build so the hardest thing for me about smoking is the weight loss. Now I keep a couple of cakes and pastries in my handbag with my Marlboros. If I'm ever tempted to give up smoking for the sake of gaining a few pounds I have a cake. Some days I might eat ten cakes but I will be happy if I have hit my daily cigarette amount."	"In the end, I realized how selfish I was being. My wife and friends were used to organizing their lives around me. Making sure we had non-smoking tables at restaurants, not using mugs as ashtrays—that sort of thing. I think it's when you start making things difficult for the people that you love that you realize it's time to start."

The Recommended
Daily Amount

Firing squads, schoolboys with elastic bands, urinating men. They all need targets. But what should you, the rookie smoker, be aiming for? Rather than just taking a shot in the dark, we suggest that you don a white coat, put your hair up in a bun, push your glasses down your nose a little and take a more scientific approach.

The Recommended Daily Amount or RDA is your guide to acting and smoking your age. But before we find an RDA for you, we need you to give us some information.

Calculate Your Daily Amount

This is easy if you know your math. First of all, write down how many cigarettes you smoke a year.

_____

Divide this number by 12.

_____

Now divide the number by 30.25.

_____

Got it? If your answer falls somewhere between 0 and 100, you will probably have just worked out your current Daily Amount or DA. Brilliant, isn't it?

Now we need to calculate what your RDA should be for your age. Use our helpful guide to get a measure of what is expected of you.

Under 5
RDA: 0
Well done for reading this at all! Perhaps your parents are reading it to you before bed. Bad news, though; you are too young. We often say in our clinics that you have to learn to walk before you can run and in your case we would like you to take that literally. But don't be too disappointed. The nipple is, of course, man's first oral satisfaction. Enjoy it (or them) while you can. As you grow up you will find you have to replace the sensation—first with pacifiers, then your thumb, then with more nipples again (or cock) and finally with cigarettes.

Ages 5 to 10
RDA: 0
Smoking is still illegal, but don't forget candy cigarettes. These have the advantage of looking and feeling exactly like real cigarettes, the only downside being that they do not contain the addiction-forming chemical nicotine. But please take note, sugar addiction is not dissimilar. The highs and lows of sugar rushes are much the same as those obtained by nicotine. Get used to this daily roller-coaster ride, it will be your friend for life.

Ages 10 to 15
RDA: 0
The powers that be still insist that you keep off the cigs at this age. You want to look bigger and cleverer than your mates and you think smoking will do this. You're absolutely right. But for now you'll have to do it the old-fashioned way, by wearing heels and reading Camus.

Age 16
RDA: 5

Hey, hey! You've made it. Happy birthday! Have a cig! Need a light? Check out your birthday cake—it's got sixteen of 'em on top.

Ages 17 to 19
RDA: 12

This is the time in your life when you'll find you get the most encouragement from other people. We call it peer pressure and it should be harnessed to whip up a lasting reliance on the leaf. You might find it hard to fit in twelve a day merely during free periods and at lunchtimes. Your school or college may even have banned smoking. This is what bedrooms were invented for and your mom won't complain if the odd smoke keeps your daily wanks down to single figures.

Age 20
RDA: 20

There comes a point when as well as acting your age you can literally smoke your age. It's the smoker's nirvana. You can't keep this up forever though! Jeng Kon Chai, at 122 the oldest woman in the world, in fact smokes only eighty-seven cigarettes a day. She's embarrassed, but you needn't be.

Ages 21 to 30
RDA: 32

This is a difficult period where many people fail. As we grow older the serious dangers of smoking come into sharp focus. It's a good idea to get seriously into alcohol during this period. You'll soon recover the gay abandon of your teenage years.

Ages 30 to 50
RDA: 40

During these two long decades you will work like a bastard to pay for romantic candlelit dinners with your mistress or boytoy, for dirty weekends *and* family vacations, for your kids' college education *and* your wife/husband's first cosmetic or otherwise essential operations. These are harsh conditions and smoking is anything but pretty. Men will cough and grunt and sweat when walking. Women will struggle to find a perfume strong enough to mask the stale smell of nicotine. Two packs of Merits will be more of a chore than a pleasure, but stick with it because...

Ages 50 to 65
RDA: 50

You can see the light at the end of the tunnel. Your only problem is how to find the time to fit fifty cigs into your day when you are still working part time and the school have told you they will find someone else to hold the lollipop if you can't leave the smokes alone when you are on duty. No problem, though, just maximize the smoking opportunities presented by your leisure time. If you have an IQ over 55, you will find that you can pop out of almost any Hollywood film three or four times without losing the plot. As for music concerts and recitals, you're well out of your punk phase by now: you could squeeze two cigs into the middle eight of anything Céline Dion or Jimmy Buffett can serve up at the Astrodome. Finally, take a look at your lovemaking. How long is it taking? Two or three hours? That's too long to go without indulging in a little pleasure. If you used to light up after you'd both climaxed, why not treat a full and steady erection as cause for a celebration in itself. And then again, and again. Sting (fifty-plus) has spoken a lot about this stop/start technique. You could get through fifteen or more smokes and then come like a horse. Think about it.

Ages 65 to 80

RDA: 75

You may have retired from your job, but don't think you can retire from smoking! Smoking is a lifetime commitment and it ain't got no pension plan, buddy.

Ages 80 +

RDA: Irrelevant

In theory you can smoke as many as you want. It's a miracle that you are still alive and we would in fact question your claim to have smoked all your life, as you should by all rights be dead. But it raises the question—how many cigarettes is it possible to smoke in one day? Let's work it out. Let's assume you rise at eight and go to bed at midnight. This gives you a whopping sixteen hours or 960 minutes of smoking time per day. On average, we're looking at six minutes per cigarette, giving us a cool 160 cigarettes as the daily upper limit that it's physically possible to smoke. Or so you may think. Many have achieved in excess of 200 simply by smoking two at once, breathing in extra hard or by smoking near a fan or in a sauna.

Barney - 51

"I guess, like a lot of people, I started cutting down when I was thirty. I didn't think anything of it. But before I knew it I was smoking fifteen, ten, and sometimes only five a day. Soon enough, I had stopped altogether and that was it—I didn't smoke for another twenty quite uneventful years! It's taken a lot of dedication over the past year, but I think I have finally got back into the habit. And a lot of my old friends have started calling me again."

Keith - 25

"The morning after I gave up I started coughing uncontrollably. My body was obviously trying to tell me something—so I instantly took it up again and have never looked back."

How to Smoke Twenty Cigarettes a Day... and Loads More in the Evening

Now comes the tricky part. If you thought you could smoke an occasional cig once or twice a day or week and consider yourself a smoker, you were wrong. You have twenty to get through before you get in from work—every day. Here's how it's done:

02:37 (a.m.)
Yes, you've been in bed for an hour but something's been nagging at you and stopping you from sleeping. Did you lock the back door? Forget to leave water out for the dog? TiVO *The Sopranos*? Oh, now you remember, you were going to smoke a last cig out of the bathroom window. (1)

06:45
First light and first cigarette. When you were single, you could have smoked it in bed. Now you need a bit more "get up and go." Perhaps there is a frost on the car that needs clearing or maybe the paper boy delivered to next door again. You'll think of something. (2)

07:40
With a bit of luck you are six minutes early for the train. If not, let's hope it's late again. (3)

08:20
Ah, the city. You feel great walking to work and tip your hat to street cleaners as you leave the parking garage. (5)

09:55
The fire escape. Time to catch up with your friends in the company on the football results or last night's *Celebrity Shoe Swap USA: The Semi Finals*. (6)

10.35
The fire escape. One of your colleagues from the Tokyo office (in town for a day of meetings) asked where they could smoke and you volunteered to show them. You are too kind. (7)

11.28
Staff toilets in the basement. No one's too bothered if you smoke down here. Besides which, only by smoking can you sufficiently relax your muscles. You are quite comfortable and there is always a three-day-old copy of *US Weekly* to read. (8)

12.20–2:10
You have sensibly organized a lunch appointment on the other side of town. One smoke on leaving the office, another coming out of the subway. A third waiting for your colleague to arrive (you were intentionally early). A fourth as a substitute for dessert and a fifth on leaving the restaurant. This is easy! (13)

3:00
Your irritability at being stuck in the office for the afternoon working on the mergers and acquisitions presentation has led to an argument with a coworker. You snap at him, challenging his "track and highlight changes" skills in Microsoft Word.

He snipes back, casting aspersions on your clichéd use of clip art in the PowerPoint slide show. It gets nasty. You offer him outside to settle it once and for all. He rises from his chair to accept the challenge. On the fire escape you both light up. It was all a ruse to sneak an unscheduled smoke! The pair of you light up another while discussing what stunt to pull tomorrow. (15)

3:55
The boss's office. Your CEO smiles and offers you a cigar from the box on his desk. You decline but take a cigarette from your pack. "I'm still serving my apprenticeship," you say with a smile. This is a tired exchange but it keeps you in a job with few questions asked. (16)

4:42
"Unbelievable! What time does the goddamn post go? Midday? Right. Who's got a stamp? No, I can't email it. It's a contract not a JPEG of a man with his head stuck up an elephant's ass. I'll take it myself. Damn it to hell. Who's got an umbrella?" (18)

5:40
Freedom! After only eighteen cigs in however many long hours, it's great to be your own man again. (19)

6:25
You are in the comfort zone. An evening of freestyling awaits you. You can pick and choose when you smoke this last cigarette of the day, but standing on the corner of your street (just out of your spouse or partner's sight) is your favorite spot. (20)

A Mental Map

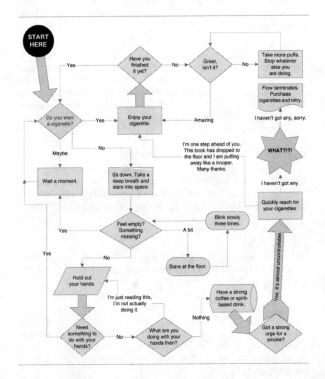

Your Smoking Milestones

Every cigarette smoked is a treat but some smokes are more special than others. You might not remember the eleventh or twelfth cig you smoked yesterday but you would be a callous person not to recall your first cig as if it *were* smoked yesterday. In this chapter we highlight the key cigarettes you will smoke in your life. These major events give new smokers of all ages something to look forward to and, indeed, to aim for in life.

First Observed Smoke

Unless you were brought up on the wrong side of the tracks and Mom's half-empty pack of Virginia Slims was the closest you got to a rattle, it will probably be a babysitter that you first see smoking. They will have told you not to tell your parents about their sneaky smokes at the playground or down at the bottom of the yard, which is advice that will stand you in good stead for your own early smoking career.

First Cigarette Smoked By You

We have dealt with this seminal moment in some detail earlier in the book, but there are those people who tried to start without reference to this manual and found the experience less than fulfilling. If you are one of those people, see "Your First Cigarette Smoked After Suffering Total Amnesia in a Serious Road Accident" for how to get it right (if you are lucky enough to get a second chance).

First Cig Smoked in Front of Your Parents

There will come a time when your parents find out you smoke, or, if you are really stupid, you decide to tell them. Either way, they won't be that pleased for the first few years. Eventually, they will come to accept that it isn't just a phase you are going through and, in fact, you are helplessly addicted. Then one day, when it is absolutely pouring outside, your dog has just died, and your mom is waiting for the delivery of a new sofa, carpets and curtains, she will reluctantly let you smoke a cig in her/your house. It's a defining moment in the maturing of the parent/child relationship, but it is still going to be a lot more pleasurable if you avoid eye contact. No one likes to see their mother cry.

Your Last Day at School

Walking out of those school gates for the last time can be truly liberating, especially if there is a newsstand opposite. On previous visits to the corner shop, you will have found your school uniform especially unhelpful in convincing the shopkeeper to sell you cigarettes, even though it's been perfectly legal for him to do so for the last six months. Now you will be delighted to find that the white school shirt covered in heavy marker pen expletives and amateurish penis drawings is an internationally recognized dress code signaling that you are indeed in the latter stages of adolescence. If only you had thought of it before!

Your First Day at Work

Your first day can be a truly nerve-racking experience. No one likes having to walk into an office full of people who all seem to be friends and know exactly what they are doing—especially now that all offices are nonsmoking by law. You will want to kill those butterflies in your stomach as soon as possible and there really is only one way for the smoker to go—straight out of the fire escape. The sense of relief when you realize you have been called into your new boss's office not to be sacked, merely reminded of the company's "one cigarette break in the morning" rule, will provide further release from the anxiety you may feel on that first day.

In Your Own Home

You've done it. You have moved out of your parents' home and taken your first step on the property ladder. Now you can sit down on a box in your empty living room and enjoy your first smoke at home. Why not use the only mug you have yet unpacked as an ashtray? You own the place!

On Your Honeymoon

We don't imagine for a moment that you will have waited all these years for your first postcoital cigarette. As a smoker, the urge to smoke after sex is overwhelming and most people will have been enjoying cigarettes in bed since their teens. If, however, you are of particularly stoic character and have managed to abstain, your wedding day is going to end with an explosion of pleasure when you've finished screwing your new spouse and finally get to light up that special cig that you have waited so long to smoke.

Your Firstborn

It is something of a tradition for new dads to light up a big cigar on the arrival of their first child, but really three or four normal cigarettes will have much the same effect. Hospital staff will encourage new mothers to wait a few hours before they enjoy their first smoke after nine long months of abstention. In actuality, however keen you are, it will probably take more than a few hours before you find the strength in your legs to make it down the ward to the smoking room at the end of the corridor.

On Film

Nowhere does smoking look better than up on the big screen. Humphrey Bogart was just a crumpled old retiree coughing his way through his favorite Lucky Strikes in real life. On the screen, he was a cigarette-toting legend. While you, as a normal, regular person of no particular talent or charm, may not make it through the auditions for drama school (let alone land the lead role in a Hollywood movie), there are still opportunities to realize your dream. You could register with an extras agency and hope for a walk-on part in the new Spider-Man. Failing that there is always *Law and Order*—although you should resist the temptation to tell everyone you know to tune in saying, "I'm the shifty-looking one in the alley."

On the Inside

Getting locked up for a stretch at some point in your life is not uncommon. The prisons are full of ordinary people who have broken one law or another. Generally speaking, there will be little to recommend your time inside. Thankfully, you are a smoker and you will at least be pleased to discover that the entire penal system revolves around cigarettes—they are even traded as currency! Imagine if your hobby wasn't smoking but numismatics (collecting old coins) and you were transported back in time to medieval Britain. It'd be like that. Your first proper smoke in jail won't really count until you have mastered the prison-yard grip—a curious way of smoking from the inside of your hand which increases the strength of the draw and, rather like drinking from the wrong side of a glass, has been known to cure hiccups.

With Your Mistress or Boytoy

At this point in your life, smoking can lose some of its excitement and glamour. With your parents dead or too old to recognize you from a few feet away, cigarettes may no longer fuel the fires of rebellion in your body. Everyone knows that you smoke and everyone expects you to smoke. They are no longer surprised when you light up between the starter and main course at Christmas lunch and use your sister-in-law's half-eaten shrimp cocktail as an ashtray. You've done it all before and it's getting to be expected of you. Having an affair, however, makes you feel young again. You will be light-headed and giddy, just as you used to be after your first few hundred cigarettes. Go a bit crazy and try smoking in every room in the house, lighting each other's while driving in the fast lane, or sneaking away from a guided tour or beach barbecue to enjoy a quickie together in the woods or sand dunes.

On Your Retirement

You have been working day in, day out in the office and now you can sit at home chain-smoking for eight hours, taking only a five-minute break every hour to pop outside and do a bit of work on the garden. Enjoy these days of freedom. After forty years or more of smoking you might not get too many.

Your Last Cigarette

It's hard to be sure exactly which cigarette will be your last. Faced with a firing squad, the cigarette you smoke as a last request will feel pretty final but, if you die of means other than execution, you are likely to go out with more of a whimper than a bang.

Over the age of sixty, it is best to think of each smoke as your last and savor every lungful. When your time is up, you can only hope it comes mercifully quickly after the last cig you smoked. It would be awful to die without having done everything in life you wanted to do—especially when the last of your Pall Malls was just over the other side of the room. It is also worth determining whether you wish to be buried or cremated. Smokers who die alone in their beds with a cig on the go may well be blissfully happy but tend not to leave too many remains—or much of a house for their families to inherit and sell off.

In the Afterlife

Clouds of Smoke

Your First Dream as a Smoker

Have you ever spent long enough abroad to actually dream in a foreign language? You walk into a coffee shop where your mother is standing in line with Clint Eastwood and the barista, (who is your old shop teacher but doesn't recognize you), asks you what you want and you say, "Cappuccino." It's amazing.

Your first smoking dream—where you appear to yourself calmly smoking a cigarette—is a crucial milestone in your becoming a smoker during waking hours. It is also a very cost-effective way to practice the gentle art. In our seminars we often invite our patients to share significant sleeping moments with the group.

Below we have transcribed three examples of the most regularly recurring first smoking dreams as they were told to us:

> I am on a train going through a tunnel when a man I don't know puts a cigarette in my mouth. I suck on it, which seems to make him happy.
>
> Diane, 27

> Every time I close my eyes I am back in the same cinema, the lights go down and the movie starts. It is *Groundhog Day* with Bill Murray. After two minutes I wake up in a sweat or screaming. When I fall back to sleep it starts again—same theater, same movie. Then, after hours of this, in one dream I leave the theater for a smoke and everything is all right.
>
> Mark, 38

I am lying on my back on the beach. My hands are digging in the sand and I feel the corner of a box. I dig it up and it is a cigarette pack—perfectly preserved under the sand. As luck would have it, I also find a box of matches with my other hand. I have never smoked before but it seems as if fate itself is telling me to. So I light a cigarette and breathe in the smoke. It is wonderful and in my dream it is so real I can taste the nicotine and smell the smoke. Then I wake up. The bedroom is full of smoke. And there is a cigarette in my hand. My mother is there shouting at me—calling me some sort of idiot.

Chris, 16

Vicky - 35

"I was sitting in the non-smoking section of my local bar and it suddenly occurred to me—"I'm not actually enjoying this!" I had got so used to sitting on my own for a couple of hours every night that I'd never actually thought about whether I liked it or not. I had a cig that evening and it was brilliant—I haven't looked back."

Billy - 45

"I was a confirmed smoker and then one day I kind of got curious and thought I'd try not doing it. That day turned into a week, then a month and I have not smoked since. I can honestly say that if you've started you should stay started, there really is no other way."

Jacqui - 25

"Probably about a year or so after I started, I realized that I'd gone for long periods of time, weeks, without even thinking about quitting. That was when I finally knew I was hooked. I thought, "I can do it—I can do anything if I want to!" I now take E on weekends and bite my fingernails. Things that I would never have dreamed of before I started smoking."

Megan - 24

"The hardest times are when I go to places like gyms or health spas. Being surrounded by temptation is really hard sometimes. Especially when you see how much other people are enjoying themselves and how healthy they look. But I stuck with it and tried to steer clear of those environments while I was forming the addiction. Now I'm so hooked that I don't really spend much time in places like that before nipping out for a smoke."

Dean - 20

"It was after my exams that I first felt like giving up. It's the times when you're least stressed that it's so tempting to throw in the towel. So I try to make sure that I'm in stressful situations or find something worrying to think about and that usually gets me reaching for another smoke."

Robin - 17

"I work in a bookshop and read your book on quiet afternoons. It was a real page turner but I didn't know how powerful it was until about six months later when my parents caught me smoking. They couldn't believe that I knew nothing about it. I had to buy the book and show it to them."

PART THREE
ON A ROLL

"I have in my hand a cigarette paper."
—Neville Chamberlain

Smoking in Public

What you do in the privacy of your own home is very much your own business. You can smoke in your underpants and let the ash drop in your lap if you want to. You can bend over naked to retrieve a lighter from under the coffee table and let the dog lick your balls. We don't care. Just pull the curtains.

Getting out and about in public, however, is quite a different matter. In 2006 and the years that follow, more and more of the country's restaurants and bars will go dark, snuffed out by smoking curfews. You can object if you want to. You can go on a march or a rally, and wave your signs at Town Hall for the mayor to ignore as he glides past in his executive car, or you can go about your social engagements with style, panache and a degree of decorum. Think of yourself as an Olympic athlete, trusted to run with the burning torch and hand it, like a baton, to the next generation of smokers (being careful to hold it in the middle and offer the butt so they don't burn their fingers). Unless you are actually standing at the counter of your twenty-four-hour convenience store short twenty cents for a pack, there is never a need to lose your dignity.

So if you are going to step out as an envoy to the smoking community you had better learn some manners. Below is our guide to etiquette when smoking in restaurants and bars (while that remains a legally permissible social act) and to the quirky customs of such places.

The first question is always where to sit or stand.

Designated Smoking Areas

It used to be the case that signs were required to demonstrate which tables in a restaurant were reserved for nonsmokers.

Now, sadly, it is the other way around. While you would once have snickered at the clean-living snobs stuck out somewhere between the screaming families and the toilets, now they are sitting together in the main dining area, chatting happily and even eating!

The Front Line

A smoker has been seated in the designated smoking area of a restaurant but at a table closest to the nonsmoking area. In fact, all that divides the tables is a cardboard sign hanging above and between them with "smoking" written on one side and "non-smoking" on the other. Sat within arm's reach of the smoker are a fifty-year-old woman and her seventy-year-old mother, who has just had a tracheotomy. An asthma inhaler is on the table in front of them. The two women are staring at the smoker—their BLTs and chips untouched in front of them. There are no rules on the front line. Just a man alone with his morality and a desperate need to smoke a cig.

The Tough Luck Club

A phrase used to describe the experience of a group of non-smoking diners who have accepted a smoking table in order to be seated at a fashionable restaurant without a two-hour wait. It never works. Smokers can smell fear. The nonsmokers will be lucky to taste the hottest Kung Pao or even see each other across the table for the sheer amount of secondhand smoke that will engulf their number like a mushroom cloud.

Once you have seated yourself, you'll then need a bit of assistance from the waitstaff.

The Excuse Me

A necessary utterance even in designated smoking areas to request an ashtray. Time was when the receptacle would be waiting on the table for you. Nowadays, the waiter will probably turn up with one sometime after the drinks have arrived. Ashtrays are also getting more discreet (by which they mean as small as is physically possible). Occasionally smokers will find the ashtray was on the table the whole time, it was just so tiny that they had mistaken it for a salt cellar or a contact lens.

The Tray Bon

The move taught to all waiters in which they replace an ashtray by placing an empty one on top of a full one. This technique was said to have been invented by Marcel Marceau for the Paris restaurant Le Lembert et L' Domestique in 1956. Up until he died, Marcel received two cents every time it was performed and bigger tips if he did it in person.

The third problem is a fundamental one—when to smoke. While no one expects you to wait until the brandy and coffee before lighting up, you should at least try to smoke between courses.

Unwelcome Break

A cigarette started but no more than a quarter smoked before the food arrives. It is generally carefully stubbed out for later, only to be swept up by the waiter with the menus.

Relight My Fire

Should the waiter leave the unwelcome break where it is, it can be relit between courses. The danger is that the smoker is now out of sync, with every cigarette smoked in two parts. It is often better to either smoke one and a half hurriedly between the starter and the main or stare at the waiter until he clears the partly smoked example away (which he wanted to do anyway).

My Apologies

The accident which occurs when a smoker mistakes a receptacle at the table for an ashtray, only to find it is a fellow diner's finger bowl for their lobster—or, worse still, their main course.

Cheeky Cig

There will of course come a time when you need to buy cigarettes in a restaurant or bar. Depending on the quality of the establishment, this can be approached in quite different ways. In a fancy restaurant or swanky hotel bar, cigarettes can be purchased from the staff and charged to the bill. This is especially useful for executives who prefer to slip the odd pack of Marlboro Lights onto their expenses.

Pick a Card, Any Card

An auto-suggestive trick played by waiters in top restaurants and five-star hotel bars. Ask for a pack of cigarettes and they will duly arrive on a silver platter with a book of house matches (see "Booker Prize," in the Glossary). The pack will also invariably have been opened and one cigarette will have been pulled out slightly from the others. This is the one the waiter wants you to smoke; best offer it to your dinner date lest it explodes.

In less impressive surroundings you will have to renew your acquaintance with the vending machine and the special tax it charges...

Brenda - 39

"I had been going to clubs and bars all my adult life but had never had a cigarette. Those nights out were quite an empty experience for me. It was like I was just going through the motions. Then I met a woman called Anne and we started seeing a lot of each other. One night we talked and talked about our lives and she asked me if I had ever tried it. I was shocked at first but after a couple of bottles of wine I was open to anything. She gave me one and my legs turned to jelly. I don't think I had ever felt such a rush of pleasure. Now my husband says I have changed and don't have any time for him. I don't know how to talk to him about it."

Paul - 18

"When I was six I really wanted to be a spaceman and I asked my mom to get me a book for Christmas on how to become an astronaut. She couldn't find such a book in our small town so she bought me your smoking guide instead. I'm all grown up now, have left home and started working as a waste disposal trainee but I recently took the opportunity to call my mom and thank her for what turned out to be such a useful present."

Concealing Your Cigarette

"Really? That is very interesting that Nepal is the same in that respect."

"The entire buffet was vegan? That sounds amazing."

"No, please carry on, I've just got something in my eye."

"Do continue, I'm just reading a text message from my personal trainer."

We all have to talk to nonsmokers some time. A few of them are actually offended if you smoke in front of them! Just follow these four basic poses and you'll be able to smoke without them noticing your cigarette. Of course, as a professional, you can spot the cigs—but they won't.

Danger Zones

You think you are doing pretty good, huh? You survived your first cigarette and moved quickly from one or two carefully rehearsed smokes a week to ten a day and then twenty. You haven't set fire to anything more important than a wastepaper bin or the cat and don't appear to have aged any more than might be expected. Doubtless you will have made sacrifices—leaving home or finishing with a long-term partner—but they have been worth it. You are a smoker. Well done. What, you are probably thinking, could possibly go wrong?

What Could Possibly Go Wrong?

Well, quite a lot, we're afraid to say. The sad truth is that just as you discover a new pleasure, the world finds ways to take it away. Ever been trapped in a subway car for three hours or spent a weekend at a health farm? As a nonsmoker, you would be frustrated and irritable in these situations. As a smoker, you will be almost indescribably MENTAL. Unable to satisfy your craving for nicotine, you will be going through cold turkey like a big dog that has found the fridge door open on Thanksgiving.

In this chapter we provide you with some smart tricks and tactics to help you through the most challenging nonsmoking situations. Think of yourself as a crack SAS commando, where SAS stands for Staying A Smoker, and you will be in the right frame of mind. Although you should note that while it is true that Who Dares Wins, in the second transport-based example Who Dares Faces A Maximum $1,000 Fine. We start, however, with a real classic.

The Weekend Spent in a Nonsmoking Household

So the deal is that your girlfriend/boyfriend/wife/husband has accepted an invitation on your behalf to spend the weekend at the country home of their friends. These people are either Mormons, Amish, Quakers or just plain squares and they are diametrically opposed to smoking. They've got the tobacco companies down on their corporate blacklist alongside McDonald's, Starbucks and the Company Store catalogue.

Your partner has never told them that you smoke so no allowances are going to be made for you. You can't possibly say no to the trip because you have just been caught having a drug-fueled affair with your partner's best friend—or for some other unarguably wrong event. You're fucked. You are in the doghouse and are just about to transfer to nonsmoking kennels. What the hell are you going to do?

First of all we have to plan your approach. These five reminders will get you off to a good start:

1. Remember to take plenty of cigarettes
You don't want to be adding sneaky trips to the store to your secret schedule.

2. Hide the packs in different places
If you get caught once, there is no shame in being caught again.

3. Don't overdo it on the journey there
Intense chain-smoking can make you feel sick. You might not actually want another cigarette for a couple of hours after you arrive and that is when you will be at your most susceptible to their clean living, smoke-free lifestyle.

4. Pack yourself plenty of minty chewing gum
If you do get lucky, it'll be your little secret.

5. Pack a few nicotine patches
Extraordinarily annoying your hosts may be, but killing your hosts will only add to your problems.

In the Two Weeks Before
If you live near to the house at which you will be staying, a reconnaissance mission is recommended. It can be beneficial to drive by or take a nighttime peek through the downstairs windows before your trip. Check how easily the windows open and whether there are security locks. Would you need a key to open them or should you pack a crowbar? Or can you get hold of a key and copy it in advance—just to be on the safe side?

If you live further away than a two-hour journey, it is not advisable to make the trip. While you might have the time and money to go, it will be almost impossible to present a plausible story explaining your presence if you are spotted.

In the House
Your partner is engaged in one of those conversations about local schools, or Orlando's training for a half marathon, or the Thai restaurant downtown where an Alsatian dog was found in the freezer. You are unable to concentrate without a cigarette. Your first thought should be to get out into the garden—on your own. Don't worry if it is raining: that's good, as it is far less likely that anyone will want to join you. Text a friend and ask them to call you back. Answer the phone and start speaking with some difficulty due to "bad reception"—all the while heading towards the patio doors

(which, you will already have noted, open when the latch is up and the key is turned counter-clockwise). Shut the door behind you as if you are concerned that your friends should remain warm and dry and not be disturbed by your call. In the garden you have two options: Hide yourself or go over the wall...

But They Live in a Flat!

No problem. Here's what you do. At lunch, eat as much of their vegan fodder as you can get down you. After half an hour start to complain of stomach problems. After an hour head for the bathroom. Once inside, lock the door and then seal the frame completely with masking tape. Open the window and do your best to exhale the smoke as far into the free world as you can. Finish the cigarette and wrap the butt in toilet paper and flush it down the toilet. Wrap the pack, your lighter and what remains of the masking tape in a sealed plastic bag and hide them in the toilet cistern. Take a large family towel and stand with your back to the door wafting the towel toward the open window. Quickly wash your hands and brush your teeth (remembering to towel dry their toothbrush). Open the door and close it quickly behind you. Walk back into the living room, place your open palm on your lower stomach, smile a little awkwardly and declare the bathroom "out of bounds" for a few hours.

Wanna join the Mile High Club? Then you'd better read...

The Long Haul Flight

These days you need a private jet to enjoy a smoke in an airplane. That kind of travel doesn't come cheap and, let's face it, if you are that keen on a smoke then you will want to save your cash for an almighty blow-out in duty free. One of the ironies of being expected to abstain from cigarettes while traveling by air is that you will probably have four hundred brand-spanking-new cigs stored above your head throughout the whole flight. Whatever the stewardess kindly demonstrates prior to takeoff, you know damn well that if one of the engines fails, or if terrorists shoot the pilot, it won't be the emergency oxygen mask you are reaching for.

If you are scared of flying, remember that it's not just you who finds the prospect of going eight or more hours without a cigarette troubling. A significant number of nonsmokers are also fearful of air travel. The best advice we can offer is: don't look down—all you will see are tiny little people smoking tiny little cigarettes, maybe even buying them from tiny little twenty-four-hour convenience stores.

It will probably take four or five hours in the air before you are suitably desperate to risk a cigarette. The fines for getting caught are very steep and you will need "the madness" not to care about the penalty. You are also going to need an accomplice and (preferably) one of the opposite sex. When we mentioned the Mile High Club earlier, we weren't joking. It is far more socially acceptable to have sex in an airplane bathroom than to smoke a cigarette. On some flights it is even quite common for the stewarding staff to applaud couples who manage to get it on in the cramped bathroom, and offenders are rarely fined for shagging. The sexual act will provide you with the cover you need to sneak this most illicit of smokes.

On the way to the toilet take care to give out the right signals. Tucking a cigarette behind your ear would be a dead giveaway. It is sexual arousal you are trying to convey. The man should "conceal" the cigarettes by pushing a pack into the pocket of a pair of tight-fitting jeans at a jaunty angle. There might not be enough pocket space for this carrying position if the man actually is aroused so he should try not to get too excited and should prepare for his bathroom trip by watching fifteen minutes of *Driving Miss Daisy* on the in-flight entertainment system.

When the bathroom does become free, be sure not to rush in too quickly. Other couples may well have been trying the same trick (for sex or smokes) and it is common for one partner in crime to leave the toilet a few seconds before the other. Jump in too hastily and you could be embroiled in a very tightly choreographed threesome. Presuming that you do get inside, your objective is to convince everyone outside that you are having sex.

The first thing to do in the bathroom is light the cigarettes. Then start with the dry humping and the moaning. Try taking it in turns to bump against the door while the other person calmly takes a few drags and then swap positions. There are two important things to remember when simulating sex in this manner. One—cigs last a few minutes longer than the average male sexual performance, so cut your smokes short. Two—on no account should the female be heard to come; apart from standing around in a graveyard with tights on holding a skull in your hand, there is no clearer sign that you are acting.

If you make it through the act without interruption you have only the walk back to the seats left to perform. This should be done with slightly flushed faces (try slapping each other if that is not already part of your sex routine) and a patently cocky swagger, which should be easy to affect given that you have just pulled off one of the most complex maneuvers of modern-day aerobatics. You should be in the Blue Angels.

Mary - 28

"I always thought of myself as a smoker but by the age of 27 I had only actually smoked eight cigarettes. I had a very poor upbringing in Detroit and my family weren't very popular so smokes were hard to come by. A year ago I met and married a lovely man of modest but sufficient means. We took the bus out to the country and smoked a whole pack together on our honeymoon."

Miranda - 62

"I borrowed your book from the library. I liked the way the last pages smelled so strongly of smoke and had such yellowed corners. It gave me hope that it really would work. Unfortunately, I dropped it in the bath, so who knows what the next person will think it will do to them!"

How to Offer Cigarettes

It's when someone asks you for a cigarette that you can come into your own as a professional smoker. Yes, you can just hold up your cigarettes and say "go for it" (see fig. 1). But what if you want to give that little bit extra? Try one of these next time you're in the field

1. Pick a Card
The classic move that we're all familiar with. One cigarette stands proud, just asking to be taken. Loved worldwide.

6. The Grab
Makes it look like you have cigs with you by the bin liner (indeed you may have). Good when offering cigarettes around large groups of people.

2. New York Skyline
A cosmopolitan move popular with the jet set. Still showing the twin towers is generally agreed to be "not a good thing."

7. Laugh It Up
Offering cigarettes on top of a "Stop Smoking Book" guarantees laughs and you won't buy another drink yourself all night.

3. Nick 'O' Tine
Make the cigarettes look like they've been crushed by smoke-hating Superman. Shows that despite this, you can both still enjoy them.

8. Going Steady
Etiquette asks that minors always offer in this manner. Also useful when offering to or by the unsteady or those who have taken of much drink.

4. Let's Party
If you've had the sense to bring out more than **twenty**—don't hide it. Perhaps you have two brands to offer your new friend? Fantastic.

9. Top Hat
Take one out and place it on top for easy access. That little bit of extra effort shows that you care.

5. Work for It
Have they asked for too many this evening? Offer as usual but let them do the hard work of opening the lid and picking out the cig.

10. Kitchen Sink
Take care to keep only cigarettes in your carton to avoid embarrassing situations where you may accidentally offer keys, pens or tape.

11. Onan's Gift
It's *easy* to forget that you must offer yourself cigarettes from time to time. How can you learn to give if you don't know how to take?

12. Cig's a Goodun'
Not easy. Balance the cigarette on your hand while doing a thumbs-up. Shows that you are 100 percent behind cigs despite the serious risks.

13. The Famine
You won't *really* have run out, but if they start to take advantage, offer them this and then say "oh dear." Sure enough, they'll buy some.

14. The Test
Who are you dealing with? If your companion even *notices* the note, then they're just playing at it. Move away to be with real smokers.

15. Shotgun Fun
One for the end of the evening. Flick the cigarette directly into your companion's mouth.

16. The Marcauex
Note how even without cigarettes, the gesture of offering them is exactly the same as the international gesture of friendship.

17. The Last Supper
Offering each cigarette as if it were your last (which it won't be) shows how much you care for your companion.

18. Let's Both Get It
Showing that you are prepared to take the same serious health risk as your friend makes it a moment to cherish.

International Phrasebook

Here's a handy suite of phrases to have with you when you are out and about sampling the smoking cultures of other countries. Let's begin with the most commonly used smoker's phrases in France. Our experience shows that you will need most or all of these phrases when stepping out in our neighbors' land.

Est-ce que, vous m'excusez pouvez me dire où le café le plus proche est?
Excuse me, can you tell me where the nearest café is?

Merci.
Thank you.

Une table pour une, svp.
A table for one, please.

Une tasse de café svp. Aucun lait ne vous remercient, je suis à un régime speciale et ne peux pas tolérer la laiterie.
A cup of coffee please. No milk thank you, I am on a special diet and cannot tolerate dairy.

Cette table semble être sans cendrier. Est-ce que je peux en avoir un, svp?
This table seems to be without an ashtray. Can I have one, please?

Je suis désolé, je dois avoir le misheard vous. Pouvez vous dire cela encore?
I'm sorry, I must have misheard you. Can you say that again?

Mais c'est Paris.
But this is Paris.

Paris. Le capital du tabagisme du monde.
Paris. The smoking capital of the world.

Depuis le moment où?
Since when?

Où indique-t-il réellement ainsi? Montrez-moi la loi.
Where does it actually say so? Show me the law.

Que vous voulez-vous dire ne le faites-vous pas noter?
Comment est-ce que je vous connais ne le compose pas?
What do you mean you don't have it written down? How
do I know you're not making it up?

Je ne deviens pas agressif.
I'm not becoming aggressive.

C'est mon Dieu donné bien.
It is my God-given right.

Droite, j'ai eu assez. Obtenez le directeur.
Right, I've had enough. Get the manager.

Incroyable.
Unbelievable.

*Oui, bonjour. Cet upstart avait inventé des lois ainsi il ne
doit pas m'apporter un cendrier.*
Yes, hello. This upstart has been inventing laws so he
doesn't have to bring me an ashtray.

Bien, je fumerai l'extérieur si je désire ainsi, merci beaucoup.
Well, I will smoke outside if I so desire, thank you very much.

Obtenez outre de mon bras! Je peux faire ma propre sortie.
Get off my arm! I can make my own way out.

Que regardez-vous?
What are you looking at?

Troubleshooting

If you have followed our advice up to this point, you should never be in trouble. But we all make mistakes. Here's how to deal with them.

YOUR PROBLEM
It's 2 a.m. and I have run out of matches and can't find a lighter.
OUR SOLUTION
Got an electric stove? Easy.
Gas grill with working ignition? Safe.
Ignition broken? A setback, but not a smoke-stopper. Your house has many hidden lights. Here are just three:

- Rip the front off the gas boiler and smash the little window in the middle with your fist. Here you will find your friend—the pilot light.
- Unscrew a lightbulb from your bedside lamp and strike it firmly against the side of the table, taking care not to break the filament inside. Put the lightbulb back in and switch on. Behold—a glowing source of a thousand lights.
- Is it nearly New Year's? Have a root through the landing cupboard and you'll probably find a few firecrackers. Carefully dismantle the firecracker to reveal the snap, which is effectively a match and can easily be struck against any available rough surface. Use the novelty toy as an ashtray, while the joke makes excellent cigarette paper.

YOUR PROBLEM
I'm twenty feet underwater and I desperately need a cigarette.

OUR SOLUTION

First, well done for taking the waterproof edition of this book with you. In 1966, Ben Runcorn of Tampa invented a cigarette that you could actually smoke underwater. However, it remains untested since submersible matches or lighters have yet to be invented. On your next dive, be sure to either plaster your body with nicotine patches or strap on a tank to supply you with a constant source of delicious smoke.

*The professional smoker is
never without his supply*

YOUR PROBLEM

It's 3 a.m., I'm nearing the end of a cigarette and I don't have another one to chain on to. The all-night gas station is over six minutes' walk away.

OUR SOLUTION

The temptation will be to smoke the current cig more quickly due to the stress. This is understandable (if you've been following this book it will be a natural and enjoyable reflex) but exactly the opposite of what you should do. You are in serious trouble, but it is no time to panic. Stop what you are doing (apart from reading this book and smoking). Ask yourself these key questions and you'll soon turn something up:

- Where did you last empty an ashtray, and had you really smoked them all right to the end including a bit of the filter?

- How long would it take your neighbor to forget or forgive you for waking him up so late on a Sunday evening?
- Would you actually do any prison time for breaking into the gas station across the road and could you afford the fine? Perhaps you had been meaning to do some voluntary work anyway?

YOUR PROBLEM
I am at high altitude and my cigarette doesn't work.
OUR SOLUTION
When Edmund Hillary reached the top of Mount Everest he was bitterly disappointed to discover that he was unable to smoke a celebratory cigarette. He was forced to make do with sucking on some frozen nicotine gum and a cup of tea made with tobacco. He never climbed again, saying, "It's pointless if you can't enjoy the moment." There simply isn't enough oxygen in the air to keep the cig lit. Either keep a lighter burning at the end of the cigarette as you smoke or leap from the nearest ledge to reduce your altitude as rapidly as possible.

YOUR PROBLEM
I'm smoking the cigarette, but I'm not enjoying it. What the hell is going on?
OUR SOLUTION
Don't panic. Here's a checklist to get to the root of the problem.

- Check the fire supply—is the cigarette lit?
- Are you smoking a white-tip cigarette? Have you lit the wrong end?
- Check the pack—have you accidentally purchased low-tar cigarettes?
- Is the health warning on your cigarette pack exposed? Cover it immediately. You will find that your box of matches is exactly the right size.

- It may not be the cigarette that is at fault. Are you receiving therapy for other serious emotional problems? Does your therapist smoke? Do you trust him? Consider changing therapists.
- You could be experiencing SBMNO.[1] Are you exceeding your RDA[2]? Congratulations—but beating your SPB[3] isn't always as easy as ABC.[4] No pain, no gain. Keep on puffing.

YOUR PROBLEM
I'm in the middle of a long car trip and no one else in the car smokes.
OUR SOLUTION
What are you doing in a carful of nonsmokers? Ask the driver to stop. Get out. Walk the rest of the way and enjoy your smokes. Do not make the same mistake again.

YOUR PROBLEM
My dog ate my cigarettes.
OUR SOLUTION
And who can blame him? They look delicious to both man and beast. However, before you put the dog down, examine his poops for a few days. Dogs don't chew and if the pooch has swallowed an unopened pack you may be able to retrieve them. You'll find they go particularly well with your hair-of-the-dog morning vodka. See also the chapter entitled "The Wild Life" later in this book.

---

1 Significant But Manageable Nicotine Overdose
2 Recommended Daily Amount
3 Smoking Personal Best
4 The first three letters of the alphabet—learned in childhood.

PART FOUR
BEATING THE
URGE TO QUIT

"We shall smoke on the beaches, we shall smoke in the fields and in the streets, we shall smoke in the hills; we shall never give up."
—Winston Churchill

Coughs, Colds and Other Side Effects Beginning with "C"

Now that you are firmly in the habit of enjoying a cigarette or two every twenty minutes, there are a few things you need to know about side effects. Nothing in this life is easy and a life of cigarette smoking certainly isn't without its trials. Ever since the day smoking went bad, smokers have quit on an ever more frequent basis. Some ex-smokers return to the fold after a few years, months or even the same day. But others don't. And it's not even as if they are enjoying a cheaper alternative. They simply remain nonsmokers until the day they die. As we know from the packs, SMOKING KILLS, but, until proven otherwise, so does a life of abstinence. You can decide not to smoke but you can't decide not to die. Think about it.

Nevertheless, the number of people quitting cigarettes has increased year on year since the glory days of the 1930s, when Depression-era lines for a pack of smokes would snake so far round the block that the last man in the line would be the tobacconist himself. In recent times, we have been moving in ever-decreasing smoking circles. Anti-smoking groups have seized upon tiny inconsistencies in the arguments presented by smokers and their friends to make it seem that "not smoking" is somehow a more positive, life-affirming choice. Is it? Heck! In times of doubt, you have to ask yourself some important questions.

> *Why did I force myself to smoke those first foul-tasting cigarettes if not to enjoy them now?*
>
> *Why have I been shelling out $50 a week all this time?*
>
> *Am I supposed to just throw that money away?*

In this second half of the book, there is one single mantra to learn and repeat. Here it comes:

WHATEVER YOU DO, *DON'T GIVE UP*

Now for the "not so good" news:

Colds

You are going to catch more colds than your nonsmoking friends and acquaintances. They are going to last longer and involve more mucus. You may want to read those two sentences again. To be sure you understand, try swapping our authorial use of "you" and "your" for a simple "I" and "my."

> *I am going to catch more colds than my nonsmoking friends and acquaintances. They are going to last longer and involve more mucus.*

If you have said those sentences a couple of times out loud and perhaps looked yourself in the mirror as you said them, then you have taken a big step toward staying a smoker. YOU HAVE FACED A FACT.

You must also prepare yourself for the sad reality that many people will delight in telling you that the reason you have so many colds is because you smoke. For the most part, and especially if the person telling you is a doctor, nurse or pharmacist, it is best to remember that they are right, nod your humble agreement and make a mental note to spend more time with musicians or comedians in the future. If, however, you are up for a challenge and the person talking to you doesn't seem particularly bright you might wish to return with the following argument:

> Colds are viral infections, passed from person to person. Although it is hard to disagree with your point, you might want to ask yourself why it is that, as a nonsmoker, you catch so few colds. Why are you so unpopular? What is wrong with you? Is getting crabs now and again a good reason to never have sex, or a sad excuse from someone who can't get laid? Catching a cold is simply a side effect of leading an active, sociable life full of friends, lovers and laughter.

It is well worth reminding yourself of all the good things that come from suffering a cold every couple of months. We have listed them below for easy reference:

- A little sympathy from a new girlfriend or boyfriend (especially if you play down the smoking factor)
- At least one day off work a month to spend at the races

Coughs

Smokers are the only people who have their own cough. Whatever their nationality, politics or sexual persuasion, smokers are a people. A people with one thing in common above all else—"The Smoker's Cough." Much like the cock's crow, the smoker's cough is a clarion call to announce that morning has arrived, or, more likely, that lunch may not yet be over. Keep your eyes and ears open and you will see smokers hacking up a hardy ball of phlegm in all manner of places: halfway up a medium flight of stairs, fifteen yards from the bus stop or even on their own doorsteps. Lady smokers with an interest in perusing the latest tableware catalogues in like-minded company will often be found at a local coughing morning—gobbing their yellow bile into otherwise purposeless articles of Tupperware.

While the world generally regards the cough as an irritant, smokers think of it more as a badge of courage than as a sign of ill health. A really seismic coughing fit can burn as many calories as a 200-meter sprint or a fifteen-minute sex session. In fact, in our advanced clinics, we have often heard the personal testimonies of couples who actually timed their intercourse to coincide with their coughing fits. One woman described to us quite colorfully how she would dig her nails in and ride her partner's spasmodic convulsions for all they were worth. Every cloud of smoke has a bronchial silver lining and coughing is clearly not without its plus points.

Other side effects beginning with "C"

We won't play games with you. It would be easy to pretend that the other side effect beginning with "C" is catarrh... or the clap. Not so, we're afraid. The "C" word is cancer and the reason for the capital letter is just that, it's a capital punishment. You might wonder why we dealt with colds and coughs first in this chapter and at greater length. The fact is that as a relatively new smoker you would be unfortunate to catch cancer before ever experiencing a smoking-related illness such as influenza or bronchitis. It is also very likely that you will endure many more bouts of cold and coughing in your smoking life than you will cancers and, until a cure is found, cancer is unlikely to be something you will catch on a regular basis. We will deal with the killer disease in more detail later, in the chapters called "Myths and Monsters" and "A Word About Death." All we will say here is that it is now widely believed that mobile phones, microwaves, asbestos loft insulation, X-ray machines, farmed salmon and department-store elevators can give you cancer. That cigarettes sit comfortably in that list is hardly breaking news.

What Science Has to Say

In preparing this book for publication, our editors at Canongate Books were a great help in pointing out the odd spelling or mixed metaphor, which we may have missed in our otherwise faultless one-take dictation of this text. We lead full and busy professional lives, supervising our clinics seven days a week, while still finding time to take vacations, race our cars together and view new properties as they come on the market. There is no shame in making the odd mistake. Generally speaking the text is as we intended it. However, our editors did feel that this chapter in particular was shifting away from our otherwise positive, inspirational and "you can do it" tone of voice. As a result it was decided that introducing a full discussion of the scientific case against smoking at this stage would depress the reader, who could, after all, have spent their money on a popular novel or a movie ticket. Therefore, in the interests of providing a quick and stimulating read, the authors refer the serious reader to the countless pamphlets and posters that can be found in doctors' offices and waiting rooms around the country. Such materials may not be as well written as this book, but they do deal in indisputable facts and often include the most astonishingly graphic images.

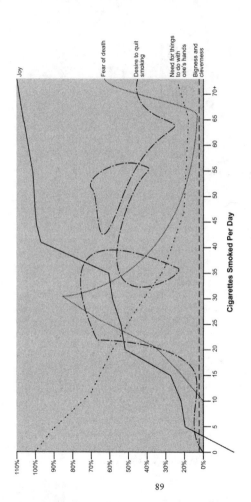

How Does the Daily Amount Affect
Key Life Factors?

How to Argue with Nonsmokers and Win Every Time

You will have read earlier how we suggested you tackle an opponent suggesting that your sniffs and snuffles are in some way smoking related. In this chapter we will discuss more advanced arguing techniques.

It may come as a surprise but the people who win the most arguments are often the best listeners. You can't possibly even begin to argue until you have heard clearly what it is that you are opposing. That is our first rule:

1st rule: Listen up. (Take notes if it helps.)

Remarkably, as an immediate result of following this simple advice, you will find yourself involved in far fewer arguments. Please excuse this brief diversion into advanced semantic logic, but if "winning an argument" can also be defined as "not losing an argument" (we can afford to dismiss dead heats and "agree to disagree" results), then it can be established that the surest way not to lose an argument is not to have one at all. On that basis, it is more common sense than academic logic that gives us our second rule:

2nd rule: Never start an argument.

Research studies have proven that whoever starts an argument is statistically unlikely to emerge as the winner. Thus far no one who has doubted the validity of these findings has managed to challenge them successfully, which rather proves the research group's point.

Listening well and refusing to start arguments really will cut down the number of disputes you are engaged in. On the rare occasion that someone starts on you and is clearly saying something you disagree with, we urge you to consider our third and final rule:

3rd rule: Maybe they are right.

You don't have to take everyone on. There are some people you really don't need to argue with. A consultant doctor in a busy hospital has far more important things to be doing than haranguing you about your smoking habit. Do him and his "real" patients (the crash and third-degree-burns victims) a favor and simply walk away. Sure, he'll shout after you down the corridor, but you have to be strong enough not to turn around and face him. Of course, it isn't just important people who are not worth arguing with. Would you enter into a debate on any subject with a tramp? Surely your time is more valuable than that. If a dog snarled at you, would you stop to wrestle with it?

At this point, you may be beginning to think,

> *Hang on a minute. This book is brilliantly written and undoubtedly represents a breakthrough in self-help books, but I love a good slanging match—a bit of verbal jousting. You promised to show me how to argue with nonsmokers and win every time, not how to look like a twat.*

But now you are starting to argue with us. It seems clear that it is probably you that has the problem. You are trouble. We are certainly not fans of nonsmoking types but on this occasion we would have to side with them. If smoking doesn't relax you and put you in a suitably philosophical frame of mind, then maybe you are doing it wrong. Try closing this book, putting it down and picking it up again. Reread it from page one.

KicK Start
POWERPHRASE Card

You never know when doubt may strike.
Cut this page out and keep it with you at all times. If you are
ever in trouble, simply choose one of these PowerPhrases
at random and calmly shriek it out in your loudest voice.

I only REALLY need one lung.	Whatever I do, I will never give up!	Who needs another 6 minutes anyway?
What do I want? A cigarette. When do I want it? NOW	I smoke when I drink. And at ALL OTHER TIMES.	It *is* a smoking matter.
I DO enjoy the taste.	3 words: GIMME A SMOKE	It might kill me. It MIGHT kill me. MIGHT.

PART FIVE
THE FREESTYLE YEARS

"I smoke, therefore I am."
—René Descartes

Reaping the Rewards

My, how your life has changed! Here we look at four key areas where you will already have improved as a person.

Sex

Where once you might have known the names of the people seated near you at work or standing at the bar in your local bar, you now count them as friends. You may not look very different to the sad loser who, just a few weeks ago, lacked the strength of character to spark up a single smoke—but suddenly everyone wants a piece of your action. That cig in your mouth lends you a devil-may-care-about-how-much-it-costs-and-how-soon-I-will-die-from-cancer look, which is so attractive to the opposite sex. Even better, if you let the cig hang from the left side of your mouth, the plumes of smoke obscure the hairy wart on your temple that used to so undermine your confidence.

Weight Loss

And boy, aren't you looking slim? Smoking and eating are not happy bedfellows. People who give up smoking often remark how quickly they put on the pounds after giving up. Not that anyone should be surprised—if they lacked the willpower to stay smoking they are hardly likely to be able to resist the huge marketing spends of Mr. Kipling and his friends. But you don't have to worry about that. You'll be having starters as main courses and dessert will be something you smoke over a double espresso. Those thirty-six-inch-waist jeans that used to cut off the circulation to your feet are now hanging around your knees like clown pants. Don't throw them out just yet—they are perfect for carrying multiple packs of cigarettes. Just roll the waist band over a few times and put seven or eight packs in each pocket and they'll fit like a pair of Daisey Dukes.

Generosity

Doubtless you will have started smoking for purely selfish reasons. Indeed, it is the only way. However, you will be pleasantly surprised or certainly not that bothered to discover that your new habit is actually helping to improve the lives of others almost as much as your own. If you are smoking just twenty cigs a day that will be an outlay of nearly $50 a week. At least $40 of that total will be going straight to the government in tax. Depending on the ethos of the ruling party, you could be funding public health care or providing valuable guns and ammunition to right-wing militia groups all around the world. Almost every time you light up, another child will be saved from meningitis by a speeding ambulance or just simply fitted with a brace by a dentist. They might not thank you now but in five years' time they'll be flashing you a smile of lovely straight white (or yellowing) teeth. You don't have to join the armed forces to feel a rush of pride when a heat-seeking missile strikes within an inch of its target or when an enemy soldier is shot in the face.

Humility

Playing such a key role in society can be a cross to bear. When a nonsmoker asks you not to light up so close to his family on the beach (because the wind is blowing the smoke in his children's eyes), it might be tempting to snatch back the state-funded nursery places that they so enjoy. But you should be humble. You may be paying for the rapacious progress of Western capitalism but you don't need to be so self-centered as to take all the glory.

How to Extinguish Cigarettes

We all hate doing it, but it has to happen eventually. In extreme circumstances, it happens before you have finished the cigarette. But it's as certain as the death cigarettes cause and the taxes you contribute when you buy them. Here is some advice on letting go and saying good-bye to your best friends.

1. The Slammer
A stiff index finger whacked against a dying cig will soon knock it out. Leaves a clean filter that can be used to filter an emergency butt rollie.

2. Own Backyard
In Danger Zones (qv) often your last resort. You may be forced to hide the pack in your back pocket, so make sure the cig is fully extinguished.

3. Michelangelo
An advanced move in which chain smokers actually extinguish one cigarette at the same time as lighting another. Not easy.

4. Out, Damned Cig!
A warning sign. If you catch yourself putting out like this, it may mean you're sub-consciously thinking of quitting. Call a *KickStart* clinic NOW.

5. Damage Control
Used in premature extinguishing situations. Flicking off the burning end ensures a maximum relight length.

6. The Bull Durham
Tying the end of the cigarette with a cord is a clean and quick solution. The flaming end is soon starved of oxygen and drops neatly off.

7. Coining It Out
Stuck at a fancy party with no sign of an ashtray or pot plant? A fifty cent coin can make a handy putter-outer. Chuck the butt in the truffle eggnog.

8. Cut It Out
Similar to the **steal** vodka and replace with water trick. Smoke two puffs off each of your parents'/child's cigs and trim them all to match.

9. The Multitasker
The original and the best. Always done with your left hand. You will be lighting a brand-new cigarette with your right hand.

10. Safety / Thirst
Worried about half-extinguished cigs starting fires? Really thirsty? It's a blazing house fire or a swig of warm tap water. You decide.

11. The Last Post
Left standing on its end, a cig will neatly burn down to a tower of ash. A potent comment to be left in nonsmokers' bathrooms/kitchens.

12. Hanging Out
Stuck at a dressy party with no trays? Just let the cig hang by your side. Soon enough it'll go out by itself. Chuck the butt in the organic guacamole.

13. The Rip Fastner
Bus arrived? No time for The Slammer, Damage Control or The Bull Durham? This will get it out and leave you with plenty for the walk home.

14. Adam's Ashtray
Stuck at the end of a lame party with no ash trays? Amaze your pals with this cool move. Chuck the butt in the bowl of vegan parsnip chips.

15. Marie Celeste
A cigarette left in an ashtray left to burn itself out leaves an enigmatic reminder of a passed moment of joy, wonder and serious risk.

Myths and Monsters

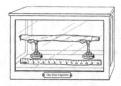

The first cigarette

A classic myth surrounding cigarettes exists in the general disagreement over whether smoking is cool. Unlike the cancer question, there is probably no way to arrive at a definitive answer to this question.

Q: Is smoking cool?

The question is most often debated by teachers and their cheekier pupils and by parents and their children. Taking even the most objective and detached view of this issue, it is hard to ignore the fact that the vast majority of people who hold the view that smoking is not cool are themselves not cool, and that the people who think that it is cool are cool. If you have followed this semantic argument, it should be noted that back in the eighties, opponents of smoking would often say that it was "not big or clever" and they actually were often both big and clever—just not cool.

In recent years a new question has arisen, set once again to firmly separate the hipsters from the bell-bottoms:

Q: Is secondhand smoking cool?

Secondhand smoking is, for those of you who have not encountered the phrase before, the business of breathing in someone else's cigarette smoke. It's freeloading, by any other name: the best way to fill your lungs without spending $8 a day for the pleasure.

Secondhand smoking is perpetrated by the same penny-pinchers who read over other people's shoulders on the train or who deliberately sit themselves opposite wealthy business-men in lap-dancing clubs to get an eyeful of free cleavage while the paying client is distracted by having a big ass squeezed onto his face. They are the same types who hang out with gay people hoping some of their wonderful homo-humor and colorful dress sense will rub off on them. Not for nothing are secondhand smokers called "Cig Hags" in smoking circles.

Nowadays secondhand smoking is big news and suddenly seems to affect everyone from grannies to children. This is despite the fact that smokers themselves have known about the benefits of secondhand smoking for years. Why else would they crowd together on fire escapes and on the front steps of buildings to smoke? They are busy professional people working in frenetic city offices and cannot afford the time to have more than one cigarette every twenty or so minutes. By huddling close together, they get to smoke their own cig and a little of everyone else's, too. Although it should be noted that the more people there are in the group, the more each member has to share.

Q: If someone can secondhand-smoke 5 percent of someone else's cigarette, how many smokers need to group together for each of them to smoke two cigarettes in the time it takes to smoke one?

In answer to the question "Is secondhand smoking cool?" the honest response is no. Standing next to George Michael didn't make Andrew Ridgeley cool and it won't help anyone who hasn't got the nerve to buy their own cigarettes either. No one likes a cheat—whether they are copying answers from the smartest kid in class or hanging out around the back of the bike sheds with the tough kids sucking up their smoke.

Below are some more smoking myths and questionable questions. Use your common sense to separate the true from the false.

- Should postcoital cigarettes be smoked before marriage?
- Should I give cigarettes to the homeless or will they just swap them for booze?
- Do schoolteachers wear nicotine patches on their elbows?
- While smoking makes men look suave and sexy, why do women with cigs on the go look cheap?
- Do the upper classes really smoke salmon?

A Smoking Technique for the Expert Smoker

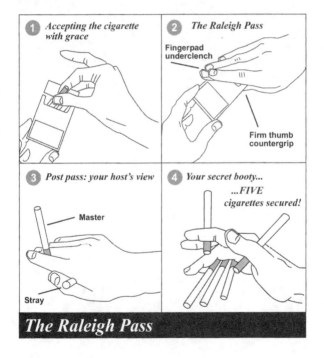

1. *Accepting the cigarette with grace*

2. *The Raleigh Pass*
   Fingerpad underclench
   Firm thumb countergrip

3. *Post pass: your host's view*
   Master
   Stray

4. *Your secret booty...*
   ...FIVE cigarettes secured!

The Raleigh Pass

PART SIX
AGAINST ALL ODDS

"You might as well face it, you're addicted."
—Robert Palmer

A Life in Opposition

This is a free country. Or is it? No one likes to think of themselves as a pawn in a game of political chess, but as a newly committed smoker that is the hand you have been dealt. You are a smoked salmon swimming upstream and the tide is flowing the other way.

Fancy turning on the TV and watching some cigarette commercials? Forget it, Castro, the days of revolution are over. The government may not yet have banned smoking completely but they are doing their utmost to make it as miserable an experience as possible.

We have already seen the exquisite art direction of the classic cigarette packs bowdlerized by thick black health warnings. It's like getting all dressed up in a bespoke three-piece Savile Row suit and then pulling a "Frankie Says" T-shirt over the top. Worse still, the copywriting on the packs has lost much of its charm. British cigarettes Dunhill Lights once offered their "distinctive bevel-edged pack" to "enhance the gentle art of smoking"—now they simply promise to KILL YOU. It's a bevel-edged coffin you hold in your hand.

Sitting on the Opposition Benches

In recent months, public smoking bans have been sweeping the country like forest fires. Headlines suggesting that the government is driving smokers underground are far from exaggerated (although not completely accurate: smokers will be quick to remember that the subway way one of the first public places to suffer a ban). It's no wonder that young moms can only find the time or space to smoke their Virginia Slims while pushing their double strollers through crowded shopping centers or when giving their toddler a one-handed shove on the swing. Come next year, there won't be a café left in Dallas or Detroit where these moms can smoke, let alone a crèche. According to all reasonable projections, there will be more open countryside in America in 2010 than designated areas for smoking. Worse still, many of the non-nonsmoking areas will be in the open countryside, miles from a newsstand, 7-Eleven or twenty-four-hour gas station.

The Old Smokes at Home

The big question facing smokers of the future will be where to smoke. Although there will always be Amsterdam for the jet-set crew, the licensed cafés that allow smoking are full of pot-heads—hardly the kind of company one would wish for on a family smoking holiday. Back at home, smokers will be immediately drawn to the police "no go areas" in the inner cities. Unfortunately, the best properties (the ex-project apartments with three bedrooms, a balcony and view over the children's play area) have been snapped up by the pimps, the prostitutes and the class-A drug users. Crack addicts are as likely to let smokers into their dens as they are the police.

Opposing Theories

The real reason, of course, why the anti-smoking lobbies (and the government that bows to their politically correct agenda) are so determined to wipe out smoking in public is because they know it looks so achingly hip. They are all too aware that one waif-like model drifting down Broadway, stopping perhaps for a Marlboro Light and a skinny latte, will inspire scores of freshly turned sixteen-year-olds to start smoking. Enter the keywords "smoking," "conspiracy," "theory" and "unfounded" into Google and you will find pages and pages of shocking evidence. These reports actually go so far as to suggest that successive administrations have been massaging escalating unemployment figures by hiring the most unattractive, overweight and unhealthy members of society to stand around on street corners or sit in the middle of park benches and smoke cigarettes. We have been smoking for years, as have almost all of our friends, and yet few of us has ever sat in a pool of our own piss in a subway and begged for a Newport. Neither do any of our female smoking friends have beards or push trolleys of shit around. You have to ask: Who are these people?

Eating in Opposition

Banning smoking in public is not just bad news for smokers. Restaurateurs are up in arms about the legislation. By taking cigarettes off the menu they will be waving good-bye to some of their most loyal customers. It has been scientifically established that smoking deadens the taste buds—and that's just the way the catering trade likes it. Can you imagine the effect that actually being able to taste the food is going to have on just one fast-food chain?

Traveling in Opposition

Standards started to slip when the smoking cars were removed from trains. They would arrive ten minutes late and no one would complain—people would be quite happy smoking an extra cigarette on the platform. It was worse in the air. Smoking seats were removed from commercial airlines and look what happened—a huge decline in the last five years and no one wants to fly anymore. By Christmas 2001 Americans had all but stopped traveling to Europe. Incidentally, if you were wondering what exactly happened to all the smoking seats, we can tell you. We snapped them up at auction. Take a seat at one of our nationwide Kick Start clinics and you will be flying first class to your smoking goal!

Overthrowing the Government

As the packaging and price of this book will clearly have indicated, this is hardly the most serious of social, economic or political studies. If that is what you are looking for, you can send this copy to us in a Jiffy bag with a check for $29.99 (that's a savings of $5 on the published price) and we will send you a copy of *The Better Way to Start Smoking*. Our goal in this book, however, is simply to help you start smoking and keep you smoking—not to bring down the government with our incisive countercultural essaying.

In any event, we might be wrong. Time is a great healer. Can you believe, for example, that before the age of consent was lowered for same-sex couples, people in this country really thought that sixteen-year-old boys fucking each other up the ass was a bad thing? That said, this is our chance to DO SOMETHING, to fly in the face of political correctness and MAKE A STAND. If anyone goes as far as to organize a march or a concert in the park in defense of smokers' rights, you can COUNT US IN.

Smoking in the Future

Imagine life in the Middle Ages. Not a lot of fun, is it? If we were to compile a list of everything that they didn't have back then—from halogen lamps to Xboxes—it would take up the rest of this book. So let's concentrate instead on the one thing obviously missing from the life of a fourteenth-century individual—cigarettes. Back then you wouldn't have to wait until you were sixteen before you could pop down the shop for a pack of smokes, you'd have to wait until you were 416! The chances of even the keenest wannabe smoker from the Middle Ages getting anywhere near their own middle age were slim. Despite all the smoking-related illness fuss that has clouded late-twentieth-century thinking about cigarettes, the fact is that we have been living for longer and longer the more and more we have smoked. Our medical profession could learn a few lessons from history, perhaps.

Hang on, you are shouting, this chapter isn't supposed to be about the past. And you are right. It isn't. But in taking you back in our textual time machine, we have hopefully given you a sense of perspective on your own times. The fourteenth-century man in the above illustration couldn't possibly have imagined the modern-day wonders of wireless technology, space exploration and duty-free cigarettes. Can you imagine what life will be like when it's 2300? (The year 2300—not the closing time of the local liquor store.) Of course not. You can see as far into the future as the *TV Guide* Christmas listings.

We should, however, declare an interest at this point. We don't have crystal balls and can't see around corners, but we do get paid extremely well by some of the biggest tobacco companies in the world to tell them what smoking will be like in the future. So while we can't be sure that by the year 2020 ultra-light cigarettes will be so weightless that they will be sold in lead-lined packets to stop them floating off on the breeze, we can tell you that the industry has listened. And it has made notes. It is only a matter of time.

2006
Smoking is banned in all prisons worldwide, prompting a huge drop in crime on every continent as habitual criminals opt out of jail—having been made to feel like prisoners in their own homes. Only nonsmokers now bother breaking the law. In the United States, a record-low figure of three crimes will be committed in 2007. Elton John embarks on a farewell tour to the disappointment of millions of fans.

2010
Smoking in public is banned on land and in the air in 457 countries. Only France and Japan have strong enough economies to oppose the United Nations–enforced ban and weather the political and financial sanctions. A huge boom in tourism helps both countries and the Place de la Concorde is converted into a giant ashtray.

2020
The first zero-oxygen space cigarette is developed. Smoking vacations in space expected to be the next tourist boom.

2025
A beleaguered tobacco industry rallies to celebrate new statistics revealing that more people now die from cell phone–related diseases than from smoking. It's a narrow margin—16 million smoking deaths in the United States in the year 2024 against 16.25 million phone cancers. Elton John embarks on a farewell tour to the disappointment of millions of fans.

2030

The first zero-oxygen space cigarette is successfully lit. Despite the industry crash of 2020, smoking holidays in space are expected to provide the next tourist boom.

2035

A new cigarette brand is launched, requiring all health warnings to be revised overnight. Just one of the new ultra-high-tar cigarettes will instantly kill any man or woman who smokes it. Faced with years of government legislation and oppression combined with the indisputable evidence of a slow, drawn-out death from any one of hundreds of cancers or heart failure, young smokers now favor the immediacy of the killer cigarettes. Thousands die on the first day of their release.

2040

An anti-smoking pill is developed which is so effective that only the very forgetful now smoke at all. Scientists rush to introduce a morning-after pill, which being 99 percent Rohypnol erases all lingering memories of pleasure, fun and fulfillment from the night before.

2075

The first death from natural causes of a lifetime nonsmoker is hushed up by the U.S. government. Underground pro-smoking guerrilla groups refer to the incident as the new Roswell. Elton John embarks on a farewell tour to the disappointment of millions of fans.

The Handicapped and the Helpless

You will recognize the thought process. You are walking down Main Street on a drizzly Wednesday afternoon on your way to take a bag of change from work to the business counter at Citibank.

You pass a Dunkin' Donuts and think you might like a doughnut or a cruller. There is one table outside, partly sheltered from the rain, where a woman in a wheelchair is sitting with a caring if somewhat dour-faced older woman. On the table is a small, round tinfoil ashtray half full of rainwater on which three cigarette butts are floating. The older woman is lighting a fourth cig for her disabled companion.

And you think—that's the life, that is. Enjoying the perks of the café society on a weekday when everyone else is hard at work, chain-smoking with no regard to the health risks, spending willy-nilly with no concern for tomorrow, let alone a pension plan.

Publisher's note: The remainder of this chapter was withdrawn prior to publication.

The Wild Life

Everyone knows that nicotine is the magic ingredient that makes cigarettes so damn addictive. But the ol' smokes also contain a lot of tobacco. In fact, to quite a large degree, cigarettes are made from the dried, rolled and shredded leaves of the tobacco plant. We know what you are thinking: Plants? Yeugh! No thanks. And you're right. When you stop and think about it, it does sound horrible. Thankfully, anti-smoking groups have spent years going on about all the thousands of chemicals that are packed into each cigarette, which is just what the young kids want to hear. They don't like vegetables and salad leaves. They love chemicals. Give 'em a Snickers and a couple of Es and they're off on one for the weekend.

Marketing men know all about the dangers of healthy products. Dandelion and Burdock isn't the world's most popular soft drink for no reason—it isn't the world's most popular soft drink because it sounds disgusting, tastes disgusting and has a laughably small advertising budget. The makers of Coke, which of course is the most popular beverage on the planet, describe their own product on their own cans as SOFT DRINK WITH VEGETABLE EXTRACT, but presumably only because they are legally obliged to do so. Doubtless the real reason they keep the drink's secret recipe so secret is that if anyone even began to imagine the misshapen and outlandish root vegetables being squeezed into each can, they would never touch another drop.

So cigs are made from plants. And while the fact that the twenty Winstons you just purchased are actually a product of the good earth might not impress the lads on the building site, it can come in handy if you find yourself in a vegan farmer's market arguing with a Mother-Earth-loving, macrobiotic pain-in-the-ass type of person about smoking. It's not natural, they will whine, it's a product of industrialization, a human act of chemical malpractice far worse than the atom bomb. Besides which, animals don't smoke…

We've cut their drippy, hippy diatribe off at that point for a good reason. And that is exactly where you should cut them off if they haven't fainted from malnutrition mid-sentence anyway. Animals don't smoke. Oh really? Well, maybe we know better. Animals are actually quite inclined toward cigarettes. Think about this for a minute. Everyone knows that dogs just love Pedigree Chum, but they wouldn't be wolfing it down every day if their sympathetic owners weren't around to open the tricky tins. The fact is that animals love cigarettes, cigars, pipes and cheroots—they just have terrible trouble lighting the damn things.

Evidence is sketchy at best, with most video footage being shot at night when heat-sensitive cameras can identify the burning tip of a crafty cig smoked in the dense undergrowth of the jungle or hundreds of miles into the desert. What follows is what we know about…

The Animals That Smoke

The Monkey

The opposable thumb is often cited as the reason for man's progressive dominance over other animals. It's no coincidence that it's also essential for using lighters and striking matches. A monkey can peel the wrapper off a pack of cigarettes quicker than any man. However, only a rarefied number of the species can stop themselves from peeling the paper off the cigarettes themselves. These lucky few are very happy smokers. Sigourney Weaver certainly had a secret to keep after her three months filming *Gorillas in the Mist*.

The Ant
Not much of a smoker in truth but they can lift six times their body weight, which just happens to be the equivalent weight of a single cigarette. If you think you are losing cigarettes or that your pack feels light, check the house first for teenage offspring...and then for ants.

The Rabbit
Surely everyone has seen the pictures of late-seventies rabbits smoking their way through those old-school brands. Anti-smoking and animal rights groups made the point that given the alternative of having shampoo squirted in their eyes, it is hardly surprising that so many bunnies volunteered so enthusiastically for the smoking trials.

The Ostrich
Smokers the world over admire any beast that hides its head in the sand when confronted with serious danger.

The Camel
Camels are blessed with their own brand of cigarettes but really don't need any encouragement. It's often assumed that the camel's hump is used to store water. Wrong—it is actually a gargantuan tumor. Heavy camel smokers, you will note, have two.

The Fly
We've all been forced to remember from time to time that each cigarette we smoke shortens our lives by six minutes. It's a little-known fact that detectives check the backgrounds of young people involved in murders or traffic accidents for evidence of binge smoking or unusually high consumption. But consider the problems of the common housefly. With a life span of only twenty-four hours, and then six minutes

taken off for every cigarette smoked, they'll be lucky to make it to lunchtime.

Other Animals

Followers of the Darwinian theories of natural selection and evolution will countenance only one possible smoking creature—the puffer fish. Creationists, however, take a much more interesting view. In biblical circles it is widely regarded that all animals smoked like troopers right up until the great flood. Noah's strict nonsmoking policy aboard the Ark (it was a wooden boat after all) put paid to all that.

PART SEVEN
GRADUATION DAY

"*Reader—I smoked it.*"
—Jane Austen, *Pride and Prejudice*

So You Think You're a Smoker?

A time to reflect on lessons learned. If you're not on at least thirty a day at this point, then go back to the beginning and reread the entire book. These exercises will help you determine if you really have cracked the habit. There are ten questions below. You should answer them all.

1. It is 3 a.m. You have plenty of tobacco but have run out of Rizlas. All the shops are closed. What do you do?

A) Make some butt roll-ups.
B) Chew the tobacco.
C) Search out a copy of the Bible—certain that its thin leaves are made from the same stock as cig paper—and make your own glue from flour and water.

2. When you step up to the counter of your local newsstand, the first thing the assistant says to you is:

A) "Twenty of the usual?"
B) "Sorry buddy, I legally can't sell it to you before 11 a.m. There are some liqueur chocolates on the bottom shelf that might keep you going."
C) "That's four packs a day to the door this week plus those Rizlas you woke me up for on Thursday night—$173.53 please."

3. It is the end of a wonderful dinner at a restaurant with a new lover. She/he asks you for a cigarette. You have seven cigarettes left. But you want one for now, one for the walk to the bus stop, one for waiting for the bus, one for the stairs up to the flat, one for in bed and two for the morning. Do you...?

A) Give her a cigarette. You can just about make do with only one in the morning.
B) Pretend you misheard her and agree that the pirouette is the most delicate of all ballet moves.
C) Dump her.

4. Which is the best cigarette of the day?

A) The first.
B) The one after dinner.
C) Do not force me to choose between my children.

5. While you are leaning to flush the toilet your cigarettes fall out of your top pocket and into the toilet bowl. Do you...?

A) Flush them away and move on to the pack of cigarettes in your back pocket, making a mental note to buy some more.
B) Carefully pick them out, discarding any soaked ones but salvaging those that are at least partially dry by laying them out on toilet paper.
C) Watch in awe as your arm instinctively whips forward like a lizard's tongue and grabs the cigarettes before they even hit the surface of the water.

6. Where have I hidden your cigs?

A) That's not funny.

B) Hopefully, by complete fluke, you hid them in exactly the same place as I left them or you could be in trouble.

C) Even if you gave them back to me right now with a full apology and a $300 donation to a charity of my choice, you would be shot twice in the back as you walked away.

7. Your house is on fire. What do you rescue first?

A) Your grandfather's antique platinum Zippo.

B) Your grandfather.

C) My house is packed so full of cigs that it would be a pleasure just to stand next to the burning building and breathe deeply.

8. You have to take a five-hour SAT examination with no prospect of a cigarette break. Do you...?

A) Study exceptionally hard while smoking your regular amount, complete the exam in thirty minutes and then run outside for a smoke.

B) Tally up each cigarette you would have smoked at the top of the paper like days spent in prison chalked on a cell wall.

C) Skip school that day and resolve that all the real answers in life can be found at the bottom of an empty cig pack.

9. You have smoked your last cigarette and need to buy some more but only have $1 to your name. Do you ...?

A) Pull out the sofa cushions in the hope of finding a couple of quarters, a half-smoked pack of cigs or an unclaimed winning lottery slip.

B) (Depending on your age and circumstances) raid your mother's purse or smash open your kid's piggy bank.

C) Go out and get a job—THIS CAN NEVER HAPPEN AGAIN.

10. You are driving down an empty road at night when the only other vehicle, a Mack truck carrying a load of 800,000 Camel cigarettes, swerves off the road—killing the driver instantly. Do you ... ?

A) Call the police and stay with the vehicle to ensure that no one gets their hands on the contraband booty. That kind of volume being shifted at fleamarkets could wreak havoc with the cost of a regular pack of smokes.
B) Wait patiently in your car for a few hours to see if another truck carrying a better brand of cigs does exactly the same thing.
C) Work through the night, loading up your car and dropping them back home, before checking that the driver wasn't about to take half a pack to the grave.

Mostly As
You really should consider turning back the clock by three weeks and reading this book again right from the very first page. If you have made notes in the margins in pencil then rub them out. If you have used ink, it is probably best to give this copy to the Salvation Army and buy another one. You have to accept that something has gone wrong. You may be going through the motions of smoking thirty a day but neither your heart nor your head is really in it.

Mostly Bs
There is no need to panic, but it is time to accept that you may have an attitude problem. Not a bad attitude problem but not a good attitude problem either. If you started your habit with the aid of hypnotherapy, now would be a good time to

reread the small print and the customer testimonials on the hypnotist's brochure. If you have been eating onions as if they were apples and taking your clothes off every time you hear the *Friends* theme, you may wish to consider booking a more private one-on-one consultation next time.

Mostly Cs

Hello, friend. We are speaking to you now as a near equal. All you have to worry about is that you don't get too cocky. We didn't write the rest of this book just to massage your ego. In our clinics we have had patients who have accelerated to smoking over sixty a day within less than a month of starting and who quickly burnt out (in fact, one of them died a year later). So be humble, keep your head down and stick with the program.

The Smoker's Pledge

I _____, do solemnly swear, on this being the first day of the rest of my smoking life, to henceforthwith smoke continually without pause. Whence ever anyone, anywhere, reaches out for a cigarette, I will ensure my pack of not less than two cigarettes is proffered without fuss and for that I am responsible. I have admitted that I was powerless without nicotine and that my life had become unmanageable. I have come to understand that only addiction, a greater power than myself, can ensure that I smoke every day. I have made a decision to turn over my willpower to the care of addiction as I understand it.

I now do on this day declare to adhere to these here twelve steps in my road to discovery:

1. I know only that I will smoke today, that I will smoke tomorrow and do humbly place my destiny into the hands of addiction.
2. I, being of sound mind, will undertake henceforth not to purchase those cigarettes that are sold in soft packaging unless I am presented with no alternative by the vendor.
3. From this day forth I will not, when copping a drag of a friend's smoke, leave the end soggy nor will I inhale upon it so hard that I pass him back what does look like a smoldering carrot.
4. I will not knowingly extinguish any unfinished cigarette in such a fashion that it may not be relit by a less advantaged smoker.

5. I solemnly undertake to have a float of at least fifteen cigarettes about my person at all times for my own use and even when in the company of others who profess not to smoke to have an additional pack for when they fancy a cig after a drink or two. I further undertake not to mock or criticize their amateurish technique at this time.

6. I promise to smoke the strongest cigarettes that, to the best of my knowledge, I can physically endure and undertake not to smoke any of those the strength of which are lighter than that of the Parliament Light.

7. I promise not to bring smoking into disrepute by being seen in public smoking and crying at the same time.

8. I will not in sobriety turn one of my cigarettes upside down nor tap the end of the cigarette on the pack before lighting it.

9. I understand that by law I may not in the presence of others deny the fatal dangers of smoking but that I am permitted to raise my eyebrows as if to suggest that I am not entirely convinced.

10. I undertake to make no trips to countries outside the United States without returning with as many duty-free cigarettes for me and my buddies as can be legally conveyed by any method of transport.

11. I politely ask that other folks who have not taken this chosen path to dependency thus forward do not throw a fit or hassle me when I light up near them or their kin.

12. I will not attempt to teach my dog to smoke.

Mantra

Addiction, grant me strength that I may do thy bidding henceforth in all matters of day or night that I shall be smoking always. I open my mind for you to override my real and present fears of fatal diseases and slow and painful death. Grant me the serenity to accept the cigarettes I cannot smoke, the courage to smoke the ones I can, and the wisdom to know the difference.

Addiction, I lastly thank you for yesterday's cigarettes, for today's cigarettes and may this evening bring me many more.

Signed_____ Dated_____

PART EIGHT
THE GOSPEL
ACCORDING TO YOU

"Tired of smoking, tired of life."
—Samuel Johnson

Going out? Haven't you forgotten something?

DON'T FORGET YOUR CIGS

t's easy to leave home without your cigarettes. Don't run the risk of being stuck in an area without a convience store or twenty-four-hour garage. Take your cigs every time. Ask for a leaflet at reception.

THE LIGHT OF YOUR LIFE

SMOKE BEFORE YOU DIE

Nearly one in four of us will die before having smoked a cigarette. There are only so many packets you can hide away for a "better day." Today is the day. Ask for a leaflet at reception

The Kick Start
Seminar Script

Because we no longer have sufficient funds to pay the fines and bails we incur as penalties for advertising our clinics, the strongest promotional cigarette in our pack is now the roadshow seminar.

The seminar is our most effective teaching method. If, for some reason, you cannot attend one, we have printed below a stage transcript from a presentation we made in San Diego a few years ago.

Kick Start Your Smoking with George Cockerill and David Owen

San Diego Convention Center March 18, 2004

Preshow announcement over PA:
Ladies and gentlemen, the show is about to begin. We have been asked by the management to remind everyone that smoking is not permitted anywhere in the building. We would ask that when we shout "Start smoking now, yeah, do it, light that cigarette! Do it now! Smoke! Now!," you hold that thought until we can gather outside after the presentation. Thank you and enjoy the show.

House lights go down. "Smoke on the Water" is played loud. A seven-foot-high cigarette pack is lowered onto the stage, surrounded by smoke (dry ice). The lid of the pack slowly opens. The pack is full of delicious cigarettes. But two of them look odd—what are they? They turn around—why, it is your hosts! A lift powers them upward as they rise out of the pack to applause and cheers.

David:
Cigarette, George?

George:
Thank you, David. I'll have two.

David:
Want to borrow my lighter?

George:
No need.

George lights his cigarettes with a magician's flare plucked from thin air. (This always gets gasps and rounds of applause.)

David:
Seriously, though, welcome friends. Welcome to the first day of your smoking life. Over the next thirty minutes you are going to learn—

George:
THIRTY minutes?

David:
It's OK. There's a cigarette break coming up in ten.

This always gets a big laugh.

David:
Over the next thirty minutes you are going to learn—

George:
Wait, David!

David:
What?

George:
Look! There in the front row! I see a nonsmoker! Am I right? Am I right? I am! Can I ask you to stand up, sir? Thank you. What's your name? Steve? OK Steve, where are you from? San Diego? San Diegooh!

Note: It is inadvisable to then say the name of their home town back to them, ridiculing their local accent.

David:
Cigarette, Steve?

The member of the public will look confused, embarrassed and disappointed.

David:
Only kidding. There's plenty of time.

George:
He's just nervous because he hasn't had a cigarette yet! Right—I'm gasping. I'm popping out for a wheeze. I'll leave you in the capable hands of Mr. David Owen!

Much applause. George leaves the stage. "Yakety Yak" plays loud as David walks over to take up a position at the lectern. The lights dim and we see the first PowerPoint slide.

David:

As Billy Joel nearly sang, "Who's going to start the fire?" It's a good question from one of America's finest singer-songwriters. Who is going to light the paper of your smoking life? The dynamite that will explode your mind? Who is going to fire the pistol at you and start you off smoking? Who has the power to keep you smoking? Who has the wit, the strength and the creativity to maintain a daily smoking amount of dozens of cigarettes? Who holds the key to a life of nicotine-fueled joy? Get your notebooks out, because the answer is written on the next slide.

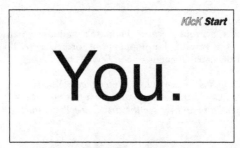

David:
That's right. "You" isn't just the twenty-first letter of the alphabet—it is also the person sitting in your chair right now, wearing your shoes and stroking your chin.

"But I'm too old to start!" I can hear some of you saying. Tell that to Rene Baumgarten, who at the age of eighty-four went from ZERO a day to OVER THIRTY a day within six months. Unfortunately you will have to wait until you are in a better place to tell that to Rene, as he sadly died from smoking-related illnesses at the age of eighty-five. But you get my point. Silver smokers should not feel alone—we have a regular session every other Tuesday that is entirely dedicated to the mature puff.

"Yeah right, pal!" I can hear you thinking. "Yeah right, you would say that, you make the green stuff off of people smoking. Get off the stage and go home now." Well, let me tell you—we have done extensive scientific research on both sides of the argument. So let's be even-handed about this and take a look now at the benefits of not smoking:

David:
(He shouts to above the gallery) Hey Simon, is the projector broken? There doesn't seem to be anything written on this slide! You say what? It's all fine, you say? Well, either the projector has broken or THERE ARE ABSOLUTELY NO ADVANTAGES TO NOT SMOKING. At this point, I must just nip out for a quick cigarette and pass you on to my colleague George, who is looking very refreshed and alert after what was doubtless one sweet, sweet puff.

George:
You got that right.

They slap a high five.

David:
How many did you get down?

George:
I banged off about eight.

David:
First class. See you later. I'm off to spend a few minutes with some very good friends.

David leaves the stage to much applause. "Smoke Gets in Your Eyes" begins to play. There now begins a short piece, without dialogue but accompanied by the music—done as if in a silent film. A simple set of a smart bar or club has been set up stage left and the lights come up to show George sitting there looking blue. Enter some men and women, dressed smartly, smoking and moving in an exaggerated contemporary style—this is almost a dance. George looks left and right. All around him are smokers. He looks out and shrugs like a sad clown. Then he puts his head in his hands and shakes his shoulders as he weeps. One of the party people, with the head of a wolf and dressed entirely in white (apart from some cork-colored knee-high boots), circles his way over to George. He taps George on the shoulder. George looks up. The party man opens his coat. Inside its lining hang dozens of cigarettes. He is like a human cigarette counter. George reaches forwards. "BANG!" There is a sharp orchestra sting as he flinches back—he can't quite take hold of the cigarettes. He tries again, and "MAH!"—another orchestra stab as the wolf snaps at his hand—another failed attempt. David comes on dressed entirely in blue with the Kick Start logo on his chest and back. The music changes to "Eye of the Tiger."

A Word About Death

Sorry.

Glossary

Aunt Sally
Name given to a cigarette requested from a fellow smoker but kept for smoking later. Example usage: "So I gave him a cig and the bastard Aunt Sallied it."

Baby on Board
Once-popular bumper stickers that now serve as dashboard safety reminders for smokers who drive and might otherwise be tempted to flick their burning butts out of the window. Two times out of a hundred, the butt will fly straight back in through the rear passenger window and torch the child.

Backburner
A cigarette accidentally placed in the mouth the wrong way around and lit.

Booker Prize, The
Kudos awarded to anyone in possession of a book of matches in which all have been lit without being removed from the book. This difficult procedure involves opening the book, folding the match over so that the phosphorous tip touches the rough strike strip and rubbing it under the pad of your thumb ten times in a row without burning off the skin.

Busman's Holiday
Term used by actors to describe landing a smoking part in a play or film.

Cancer
Terminal disease with slow and painful death caused by smoking cigarettes. Avoid.

Choking Hazard
Official term for a cigarette offered to a child who would technically be too young to know not to eat it.

Double Dutch
See **Dutch**.

Dutch
In smoking terms, the word used to describe the offer to purchase a single cigarette from a stranger when it is fully expected that even if the cigarette is given, the financial offer will be politely declined. A *Double Dutch* is when the person asked says, "OK, that's twenty-five cents, thanks." It is not advised to try the Dutch without the requisite change just in case a Double Dutch is pulled on you. In that instance, it is better to beg and simply ask a lot more people.

Duty Freebie
The very best time to hit on a friend for a cigarette is when they are in possession of 200 duty-free smokes. JFK, LAX and most other major airports have a viewing gallery where you can see the planes coming in.

Filter
The end of the cigarette that makes it easy to hold. It's a common misconception that it actually filters anything. The word is derived from the Flemish for "handle."

Fire Escape
You don't need to be able to jump a Harley-Davidson over a barbed-wire fence to free yourself from the dead air of a nonsmoking office

environment—just slip out the fire escape. Think about its name: "Fire" = smoking, "Escape" = escape. If you do have to break the glass, use a tough metal object like a stapler. Hole punchers are even better.

Freeway Fireworks
The glorious sight of a cigarette butt flicked from the window of the car in front on a nighttime drive hitting the road surface at a speed greater than 60 miles an hour.

Hands-Free Kit
A popular development in cell phone technology, but the cumbersome hydraulic facial harness designed for smokers has proved off-putting to all but the completely paralyzed.

Haringey
The origin of the name is unknown even though its introduction into popular parlance is relatively recent. "Haringey" is the word used to describe a pack of cigarettes which has been placed, provocatively or simply without thought, on a table in a nonsmoking train carriage. The presence of a Haringey on a crowded train will cause conservative male types to bristle at the prospect of a potential incidence of antisocial behavior and possible blustering argument.

Haringey Gambit
A well-positioned pack of cigarettes can, for reasons described above, keep the seats next to and opposite the potential smoker free for the duration of the journey.

Jimmy[1]
Smokers' slang for an Aunt Sally which is specifically placed behind the ear.

Jimmy²

Smokers' slang for a cigarette taken from a freshly opened pack, turned upside down and saved until last for good luck.

Jimmy³

Smokers' slang for the catch-all use of the word *Jimmy* to describe any hitherto unnamed element of smoking practice or paraphernalia.

Kindling

A small collection of dry twigs carried in the pockets of smokers fearful of not having a light after missing the night bus and walking home from a club alone.

Lip Service

The ridiculous art of appearing to smoke without actually inhaling. President Clinton reportedly paid "lip service" to a joint while in college. Practiced by schoolgirls and painfully bad actors (or exceptionally good actors playing schoolgirls), the technique involves drawing the smoke millimeters into the mouth and quickly pushing it back out by making a silent "p" sound with the mouth.

Manna from Heaven

Hiding a cigarette in your hair and making someone focus on your hands while you tip your head forward. The cigarette appears to fall from God. "It would be an insult to the Lord not to smoke it."

Matchbox Ashtray

A matchbox which provides a makeshift ashtray. Care should be taken to empty the box of unused matches unless you are aiming to effect a "genie" (playground pyromaniac slang for torching a whole box of matches).

Modern Art

Remember those enigmatic and suggestive posters in the seventies and eighties? They were ads for Lucky Strikes.

Murphy's Tea

The result when a glass of water is used as an ashtray. The water takes on a dirty brown color. Worth tasting once.

One-Toke Smoke

Seriously impressive trick in which the smoker starts and finishes a cigarette with one long drag. Rarely performed as it requires extra-ordinary lung capacity, which is in short supply among smokers. Circus owners and promoters will often approach Olympic swimmers who have recently hung up their goggles and not yet decided on their next career to perform the trick for huge sums of money.

OTBs

The minimum bet in most OTBs is just $2. This is a small price to pay to spend some quality time in this smokers' paradise. These places act as drop-in centers for lonely smokers—although they can appear intimidating at first. Just remember to close the door after you as you enter and you'll be fine (the ashtrays are made of tinfoil and will blow away in the wind). And don't bother stealing the chipper little pens, they are so small and contain so little ink that they will have run out by the time you get home.

Penthouse Puffer

A cigarette or cigar smoked in a public lift in the journey from the ground floor to the top floor. Only billionaire businessmen can afford to risk the secondhand smoking lawsuits that each ascent provokes. Example usage: "Henry in accounts did the Penthouse this morning." "No way. You're shitting me!"

Pull

The inviting message embossed on the foil of every pack of cigarettes sold. A printing error in the early eighties led to thousands of packs having "Push" written on them—causing the needless crushing of many cigarettes. Has passed into modern usage in the phrase, "Such an easy lay. She was as easy to pull as a cigarette foil."

Occasionally, a pigeon or bat will fly into the factory and become jammed in the production line, causing the silver foil to be assembled without perforations. While the vast majority of smokers will have the strength to rip the paper unaided, some elderly women in the last days of their smoking lives will have as much fun with these foils as they do with modern-day milk cartons. Enter the community nurse.

Remmel

The line running along the side of a cigarette where the paper is joined with glue. This burns slightly faster than the rest of the cigarette, so we encourage students to get in the habit of smoking "remmel down." The remmel is licked by drug addicts not only to make opening it for spliffs easier but also to get a hit off the glue.

Rush Hour Break

A cigarette smoked illicitly in the bathroom of a train. Depending on how restrictive the cubicle is, it is possible to directly smoke half a cigarette and secondhand-smoke the remainder.

Sacrifice

A cigarette ventured after waiting far too long for a bus or taxi. The Sacrifice was born of Murphy's Law. Ninety-nine times out of a hundred, within seconds of lighting the cigarette a bus or taxi will appear—probably both.

Sallue Tante

French for *Aunt Sally*.

Shoegazing

The business of picking up free smokes from the butts other smokers discard. While many people stamp out their cigarettes, others are in too much of a hurry (or just happy to hand you a lifeline). For best results, hang out by bus stops and hope that the **Sacrifice** works its magic. Generally, it pays not to be too fussy about specific brands. Shoegazing is best practiced by those who already have most major oral diseases (cold sores, herpes, rabies). Don't bother going out in, or after, rainfall—the butts will be soaked and you won't know which ones have been pissed on by dogs.

Smoking Championships, International

Held every other year in Boston, the International Smoking Championships are now in their 43rd year. Events include Quickest Smoke, Slowest Smoke, Freestyle Smoking, Remote Smoking, Stunt Smoking, Smoke Sculpture, Endurance, Triple Smoking and Smoking While Driving or Operating Machinery. Malcolm Gai (Tokyo) holds the gold medal for catching the most cigarettes in his teeth when fired from a modified machine gun. He caught and spat 4,343 in one hour, smashing the previous record by 4,342.

Stowaway

A rogue cigarette butt which mysteriously appears on the carpet in the kid's bedroom having traveled there on the bottom of a shoe, much as the smoker's husband or wife refuses to believe it. There is no point *Shoegazing* these butts—it was probably dog shit that kept them stuck to the sole for so long.

Tax

If you think you are spending $30 or $40 a week on cigarettes, think again. Likewise, if you think the war in Iraq had nothing to do with you, think again.

Teabag Cig
The delinquent child's alternative to cigarettes they can neither afford nor legally purchase. This first taste of both smoking and hot beverages can lead to two lifelong addictions. Highly recommended.

Thank You Very Much[1]
Phrase uttered with heavy sarcasm by a smoker who has graciously given a friend a drag on their cig only to have seen the guts sucked out of it and a limp, flattened cigarette handed back. This trick is often perpetrated by "ex-smokers" who have "given up" within the last seven days.

Thank You Very Much[2]
Phrase uttered with heavy sarcasm by the smoker who has politely asked a friend for a cigarette and been offered what appears to be a full premium pack to choose from, only to find later that all but one smoke had been substituted for disgusting extra ultra lights bought erroneously that morning.

Wreath
The sore lip caused by pulling out of your mouth too quickly a cigarette that has stuck to your lips on a cold day. Easily avoided by not removing the cigarette at all.